Collins

Collins
German
Words

2011

D0511271

HarperCollins Publishers
Westerhill Road
Bishopbriggs
Glasgow
G64 2QT
Great Britain

First Edition 2006

ISBN-13 978-0-00-723157-7
ISBN-10 0-00-723157-1

www.collins.co.uk

A catalogue record for this book is available
from the British Library

Typeset by Davidson's Prepress, Glasgow

Printed in Italy by Rotolito Lombarda SpA

Acknowledgements
We would like to thank those authors and
publishers who kindly gave permission for
copyright material to be used in the Collins
Word Web. We would also like to thank
Times Newspapers Ltd for providing
valuable data.

PUBLISHING DIRECTOR
Lorna Knight

EDITORIAL DIRECTOR
Michela Clari

MANAGING EDITOR
Maree Airlie

PROJECT CO-ORDINATOR
Gaëlle Amiot-Cadey

CONTRIBUTOR
Horst Kopleck

BASED ON THE COLLINS GEM
GERMAN VITAL VOCAB BY
Barbara I. Christie
Màiri MacGinn
Horst Kopleck
Veronika Schnorr

William Collins' dream of knowledge for all began with the publication of his first book in 1819. A self-educated mill worker, he not only enriched millions of lives, but also founded a flourishing publishing house. Today, staying true to this spirit, Collins books are packed with inspiration, innovation, and practical expertise. They place you at the centre of a world of possibility and give you exactly what you need to explore it.

Language is the key to this exploration, and at the heart of Collins Dictionaries is language as it is really used. New words, phrases, and meanings spring up every day, and all of them are captured and analysed by the Collins Word Web. Constantly updated, and with over 2.5 billion entries, this living language resource is unique to our dictionaries.

Words are tools for life. And a Collins Dictionary makes them work for you.

Collins. Do more.

contents

6 contents

The *Easy Learning German Words* is designed for both young and adult learners. Whether you are starting to learn German for the very first time, revising for school exams or simply want to brush up on your German, the *Easy Learning German Words* offers you the information you require in a clear and accessible format.

This book is divided into 50 topics, arranged in alphabetical order. This thematic approach enables you to learn related words and phrases together, so that you can become confident in using particular vocabulary in context.

Vocabulary within each topic is divided into nouns and useful phrases which are aimed at helping you to express yourself in idiomatic German. Vocabulary within each topic is graded to help you prioritize your learning. Essential words include the basic words you will need to be able to communicate effectively, important words help expand your knowledge, and useful words provide additional vocabulary which will enable you to express yourself more fully.

Nouns are grouped by gender, which makes it easier to remember if they are masculine ("der") nouns, feminine ("die") nouns and neuter ("das") nouns. In addition, all plural forms are shown, with the exception of feminine nouns ending in –in (these regularly become –innen in the plural) and those forms, of whatever gender, which have the same form in both singular and plural.

Nouns which have been derived from adjectives follow the style:

> Alte(r), -n   old man/woman

This means that the noun ending depends on whether the article is definite or indefinite, masculine or feminine, singular or plural. For example:

der Alte	*masculine singular (definite article)*
ein Alter	*masculine singular (indefinite article)*
die Alte	*feminine singular (definite article)*
eine Alte	*feminine singular (indefinite article)*
die Alten	*masculine and feminine singular (definite article)*
Alte	*masculine and feminine singular (no article)*

At the end of the book you will find a list of supplementary vocabulary, grouped according to part of speech – adjective, verb, noun and so on. This is vocabulary which you will come across in many everyday situations.

Finally, there is an English index which lists all the essential and important nouns given under the topic headings for quick reference.

The *Easy Learning German Words* helps you to consolidate your language learning. Together with the other titles in the *Easy Learning* range you can be sure that you have all the help you need when learning German at your fingertips.

ABBREVIATIONS

acc	accusative
adj	adjective
adv	adverb
conj	conjunction
dat	dative
etw	etwas (meaning *something*)
f	feminine
gen	genitive
jdm	jemandem (meaning *somebody – dative case*)
jdn	jemanden (meaning *somebody – accusative case*)
m	masculine
n	noun
nt	neuter
pl	plural
prep	preposition
sb	somebody
sth	something

ESSENTIAL WORDS (*masculine*)

der	Ausgang, ⸚e	way out, exit
der	Ausstieg, -e	exit
der	Check-in, -s	check-in
der	Eingang, ⸚e	entrance
der	Fahrgast, ⸚e	passenger
der	Fahrkartenschalter	ticket office
der	Fahrplan, ⸚e	timetable
die	Ferien (*pl*)	holiday
der	Flug, ⸚e	flight
der	Fluggast, ⸚e	airline passenger
der	Flughafen, ⸚	airport
der	Flugplan, ⸚e	flight schedule
der	Flugplatz, ⸚e	airfield; airport
der	Flugpreis, -e	(air) fare
der	Flugschein, -e	(plane) ticket
der	Gepäckträger	porter
der	Gepäckwagen	luggage trolley
der	Geschäftsmann, -leute	businessman
der	Koffer	case, suitcase
der	Kofferkuli, -s	luggage trolley
der	Notausgang, ⸚e	emergency exit
der	Pass, ⸚e	passport
der	Passagier, -e	passenger
der	Personalausweis, -e	identity card
der	Reisende(r), -n	traveller
der	Reisepass, ⸚e	passport
der	Sicherheitsbereich, -e	security area
der	Steward, -s	steward
der	Tourist, -en	tourist
der	Urlaub	holiday(s)
der	Urlauber	holidaymaker
der	Zoll	customs; duty
der	Zuschlag, ⸚e	extra charge

ESSENTIAL WORDS (feminine)

die Ankunft, ¨e	arrival
die Auskunft, ¨e	information; information desk
die (einfache) Fahrkarte, -n	(single) ticket
die Gepäckausgabe	baggage reclaim
die Maschine, -n	plane
die Personenkontrolle, -n	checkpoint (for passengers)
die Reservierung, -en	booking, reservation
die Richtung, -en	direction
die Rückfahrkarte, -n	return (ticket)
die Sicherheitskontrolle, -n	security check
die Stewardess, -en	air hostess
die Tasche, -n	bag
die Toilette, -n	toilet
die Touristin	tourist
die Uhr, -en	clock; time
die Urlauberin	holiday-maker

ESSENTIAL WORDS (neuter)

das Fliegen	flying
das Flugzeug, -e	plane, aeroplane
das Fundbüro, -s	lost property office
das Gepäck	luggage
das Passagierflugzeug, -e	airliner
das Schließfach, ¨er	left luggage locker
das Taxi, -s	taxi
das Ticket, -s	(plane) ticket

USEFUL PHRASES

einen Flugschein or ein Ticket lösen to buy a (plane) ticket
einen Rückflug buchen to book a return flight
hin und zurück nach Köln a return to Cologne
ich packe I pack; ich packe aus I unpack
das Gepäck durchleuchten to scan the luggage
einchecken to check in; fliegen to fly; wir fliegen ab we fly off
erreichen to catch; verpassen to miss

IMPORTANT WORDS (masculine)

der	Abflug, ⸚e	takeoff, departure
der	Duty-free-Shop, -s	duty-free shop
der	Jumbojet, -s	jumbo jet
der	Kontrollturm, ⸚e	control tower
der	Metalldetektor, -en	metal detector
der	Pilot, -en	pilot
der	Sicherheitsbeamte(r), -n	security officer
der	Sicherheitsgurt, -e	seat belt
der	Start, -s	takeoff
der	Terminal, -s	(air) terminal
der	Terrorist, -en	terrorist
der	Zollbeamte(r), -n	customs officer

IMPORTANT WORDS (feminine)

die	Autovermietung, -en	car hire
die	Bordkarte, -n	boarding card
die	Landung, -en	landing
die	Sicherheitsbeamtin	security officer
die	Startbahn, -en	runway
die	Terroristin	terrorist
die	Verbindung, -en	connection
die	Verspätung, -en	delay
die	Zollkontrolle	customs control or check

IMPORTANT WORDS (neuter)

das	Abfluggate, -s	departure gate
das	E-Ticket, -s	e-ticket
das	Flugticket, -s	ticket
das	Handgepäck	hand luggage
das	Reisebüro, -s	travel agent's
das	Reiseziel, -e	destination

USEFUL PHRASES

starten to take off; beim Start during the takeoff
an Bord on board; luftkrank airsick
ein Flugzeug entführen to hijack a plane
landen to land; verspätet delayed, late

USEFUL WORDS *(masculine)*

der	**Anhänger**	label, tag
der	**Aufkleber**	sticker, label
der	**Babyraum, ¨e**	mother and baby room
der	**Fluglotse, -n**	air traffic controller
der	**Flugsteig, -e**	gate

USEFUL WORDS *(feminine)*

die	**Besatzung, -en**	crew
die	**Besucherterrasse, -n**	spectator terrace
die	**Bombe, -n**	bomb
die	**Gepäckermittlung**	lost luggage office
die	**Landebahn, -en**	runway
die	**Rollbahn, -en**	runway
die	**Rolltreppe, -n**	escalator
die	**Schallmauer**	sound barrier
die	**Turbulenz**	turbulence
die	**Wechselstube, -n**	bureau de change
die	**Zwischenlandung, -en**	stopover

USEFUL WORDS *(neuter)*

das	**Bodenpersonal**	ground staff
das	**Durchleuchtungsgerät, -e**	scanner
das	**Düsenflugzeug, -e**	jet plane
das	**Restaurant, -s**	restaurant

USEFUL PHRASES

einen Zuschlag zahlen **to pay a supplement**
zuschlagpflichtig **subject to an extra charge**
gültig **valid**
erhältlich **available**
durch den Zoll gehen **to go through customs**
verzollen **to pay duty on**
haben Sie etwas zu verzollen? **do you have anything to declare?**
nichts zu verzollen **nothing to declare**
zollfrei **duty-free**

ESSENTIAL WORDS (masculine)

der	Elefant, -en	elephant
der	Fisch, -e	fish
der	Hals, ̈e	neck; throat
der	Hund, -e	dog
der	Tiergarten, ̈	zoo, zoological park
der	Versuch, -e	experiment
der	Zoo, -s	zoo

IMPORTANT WORDS (masculine)

der	Affe, -n	monkey
der	Bär, -en	bear
der	Bock, ̈e	buck, ram
der	Hamster	hamster
der	Huf, -e	hoof
der	Löwe, -n	lion
der	Schwanz, ̈e	tail
der	Tiger	tiger
der	Wolf, ̈e	wolf

ESSENTIAL WORDS (feminine)

die	Katze, -n	cat
die	Tierhandlung, -en	pet shop

IMPORTANT WORDS (feminine)

die	Giraffe, -n	giraffe
die	Hundehütte, -n	kennel
die	Kuh, ̈e	cow
die	Löwin	lioness
die	Maus, Mäuse	mouse
die	Ratte, -n	rat
die	Schlange, -n	snake
die	Tigerin	tigress

USEFUL PHRASES

laufen to run; hüpfen to hop
springen to jump; kriechen to slither, crawl

ESSENTIAL WORDS *(neuter)*

das **Bein, -e**	leg
das **Haar, -e**	hair
das **Haustier, -e**	pet
die **Jungen** *(pl)*	young
das **Ohr, -en**	ear
das **Tier, -e**	animal

IMPORTANT WORDS *(neuter)*

das **Horn, ̈er**	horn
das **Kamel, -e**	camel
das **Känguru, -s**	kangaroo
das **Kaninchen**	rabbit
das **Krokodil, -e**	crocodile
das **Pferd, -e**	horse
das **Pony, -s**	pony
das **Rhinozeros, -se**	rhinoceros
das **Schaf, -e**	sheep
das **Schwein, -e**	pig
das **Zebra, -s**	zebra

USEFUL PHRASES

wir haben keine Haustiere **we don't have any pets**
zahm **tame**; wild **wild**; gehorsam **obedient**
füttern **to feed**; fressen **to eat**
trinken **to drink**
schlafen **to sleep**
bellen **to bark**; miauen **to miaow**
knurren **to growl**; schnurren **to purr**
beißen **to bite**; kratzen **to scratch**
ich habe Angst vor Hunden **I'm afraid of dogs**

USEFUL WORDS (*masculine*)

der	**Beutel**	pouch (*of kangaroo*)
der	**Bulle, -n**	bull
der	**Eisbär, -en**	polar bear
der	**Esel**	donkey
der	**Frosch, ̈-e**	frog
der	**Fuchs, ̈-e**	fox
der	**Hase, -n**	hare
der	**Hirsch, -e**	stag
der	**Höcker**	hump (*of camel*)
der	**Igel**	hedgehog
der	**Kater**	tomcat
der	**Maulwurf, ̈-e**	mole
der	**Ochse, -n**	ox
der	**Panzer**	shell (*of tortoise*)
der	**Pelz, -e**	fur
der	**Rüssel**	snout (*of pig*); trunk (*of elephant*)
der	**Seehund, -e**	seal
der	**Stachel, -n**	spine (*of hedgehog*)
der	**Stier, -e**	bull
der	**Stoßzahn, ̈-e**	tusk
der	**Streifen**	stripe (*of zebra*)
der	**Wal(fisch), -e**	whale
der	**Ziegenbock, ̈-e**	billy goat

USEFUL PHRASES

jagen to hunt; to shoot
zu Pferd on horseback
reiten gehen to go riding
auf die Fuchsjagd gehen to go fox-hunting
„Vorsicht, bissiger Hund" "beware of the dog"
der Hund wedelt mit dem Schwanz the dog wags its tail
die Katze streicheln to stroke the cat

USEFUL WORDS *(feminine)*

die	Falle, -n	trap
die	Fledermaus, -mäuse	bat
die	Heuschrecke, -n	grasshopper
die	Kralle, -n	claw; talon
die	Kröte, -n	toad
die	Mähne, -n	mane
die	Natter, -n	adder
die	Pfote, -n	paw (*small*)
die	Pranke, -n	paw (*large*)
die	Ringelnatter, -n	grass snake
die	Robbe, -n	seal
die	Schildkröte, -n	tortoise
die	Schnauze, -n	snout, muzzle
die	Tatze, -n	paw
die	Ziege, -n	goat, nanny goat

USEFUL WORDS *(neuter)*

das	Eichhörnchen	squirrel
das	Fell, -e	coat, fur
das	Geweih	antlers (*pl*)
das	Hufeisen	horseshoe
das	Maul, Mäuler	mouth
das	Maultier, -e	mule
das	Meerschweinchen	guinea pig
das	Merkmal, -e	characteristic
das	Nashorn, ¨er	rhinoceros
das	Nilpferd, -e	hippopotamus
das	Reh, -e	roe deer

USEFUL PHRASES

ein Tier freilassen **to set an animal free**
ein Löwe ist aus dem Zoo entlaufen **a lion has escaped from the zoo**
in eine Falle gehen **to be caught in a trap**

ESSENTIAL + IMPORTANT WORDS (masculine)

der	Gang, ¨e	gear
der	Gepäckträger	luggage carrier
der	Motorradfahrer	motorcyclist
der	Radfahrer	cyclist
der	Rad(fahr)weg, -e	cycle track or path
der	Radsport	cycling
der	Reifen	tyre
der	Sattel, ¨	saddle, seat

ESSENTIAL + IMPORTANT WORDS (feminine)

die	Achtung	attention
die	Bahn, -en	road, way; (cycle) lane
die	Bremse, -n	brake
die	Ecke, -n	corner
die	Fahrradlampe, -n	cycle lamp
die	Gefahr, -en	danger, risk
die	Geschwindigkeit, -en	speed
die	Hauptstraße, -n	main street, main road
die	Kette, -n	chain
die	Klingel, -n	bell
die	Lampe, -n	lamp
die	Nebenstraße, -n	side street
die	Pumpe, -n	pump
die	Radfahrerin	cyclist
die	Reifenpanne, -n	puncture
die	Reparatur, -en	repair; repairing

USEFUL PHRASES

mit dem (Fahr)rad fahren to cycle
mit dem Rad in die Stadt fahren to cycle into town
er kam mit dem Rad he came on his bike, he came by bike
„Radfahren verboten" "cycling prohibited"
Radsport betreiben to go in for cycling
aufsteigen to get on; absteigen to get off
bergauf uphill; bergab downhill
klingeln to ring one's bell; schalten to change gear

ESSENTIAL WORDS (neuter)

das	Fahrrad, ⁻er	bicycle
das	Hinterrad, ⁻er	back wheel
das	Motorrad, ⁻er	motorbike, motorcycle
das	Pedal, -e	pedal
das	Rad, ⁻er	wheel; bike
das	Radfahren	cycling
das	Vorderrad, ⁻er	front wheel

USEFUL WORDS (masculine)

der	Dynamo, -s	dynamo
der	Helm, -e	helmet
der	Korb, ⁻e	pannier; basket
der	Rückstrahler	reflector

USEFUL WORDS (feminine)

die	Lenkstange, -n	handlebars
die	Satteltasche, -n	saddlebag, pannier
die	Speiche, -n	spoke
die	Steigung, -en	gradient
die	Straßenverkehrsordnung	Highway Code

USEFUL WORDS (neuter)

das	Flickzeug, -e	puncture repair kit
das	Katzenauge, -n	rear light; reflector; cat's eye
das	Moped, -s	moped
das	Mountainbike, -s	mountain bike
das	Schutzblech, -e	mudguard

USEFUL PHRASES

bremsen to brake; reparieren to repair
einen Platten haben to have a flat tyre
geplatzt burst; kaputt broken, done
das Loch flicken to mend the puncture
die Reifen aufpumpen to blow up the tyres
glänzend shiny; rostig rusty; Leucht- fluorescent

ESSENTIAL + IMPORTANT WORDS *(masculine)*

der	Flamingo, -s	flamingo
der	Hahn, -̈e	cock
der	Himmel	sky
der	Käfig, -e	cage
der	Kanarienvogel, -̈	canary
der	Kuckuck, -e	cuckoo
der	Pinguin, -e	penguin
der	Schwan, -̈e	swan
der	Storch, -̈e	stork
der	Truthahn, -̈e	turkey
der	Vogel, -̈	bird
der	Wellensittich, -e	budgie, budgerigar

ESSENTIAL + IMPORTANT WORDS *(feminine)*

die	Ente, -n	duck
die	Feder, -n	feather
die	Gans, -̈e	goose
die	Henne, -n	hen
die	Luft	air
die	Nachtigall, -en	nightingale

ESSENTIAL + IMPORTANT WORDS *(neuter)*

das	Huhn, -̈er	hen, fowl
das	Nest, -er	nest
das	Rotkehlchen	robin (redbreast)
das *or* der	(Vogel)bauer	birdcage

USEFUL PHRASES

fliegen to fly; abfliegen to fly away
ein Nest bauen to build a nest; nisten to nest
Eier legen to lay eggs
singen to sing
pfeifen to whistle
zwitschern to twitter
Lärm machen to make a noise

USEFUL WORDS *(masculine)*

der	**Adler**	eagle
der	**Eisvogel, ⸚**	kingfisher
der	**Falke, -n**	falcon
der	**Fasan, -e(n)**	pheasant
der	**Fink, -en**	finch
der	**Flügel**	wing
der	**Geier**	vulture
der	**Habicht, -e**	hawk
der	**Hirtenstar, -s**	mynah bird
der	**Papagei, -en**	parrot
der	**Pfau, -en**	peacock
der	**Puter**	turkey(-cock)
der	**Rabe, -n**	raven
der	**Schnabel, ⸚**	beak, bill
der	**Sittich, -e**	parakeet
der	**Spatz, -en**	sparrow
der	**Specht, -e**	woodpecker
der	**Sperling, -e**	sparrow
der	**Star, -e**	starling
der	**Strauß, -e**	ostrich
der	**Zaunkönig, -e**	wren

USEFUL WORDS *(feminine)*

die	**Amsel, -n**	blackbird
die	**Blaumeise, -n**	bluetit
die	**Dohle, -n**	jackdaw
die	**Drossel, -n**	thrush
die	**Elster, -n**	magpie
die	**Eule, -n**	owl
die	**Krähe, -n**	crow
die	**Lerche, -n**	lark
die	**Möwe, -n**	seagull
die	**Saatkrähe, -n**	rook
die	**Schwalbe, -n**	swallow
die	**Taube, -n**	dove; pigeon

ESSENTIAL WORDS (*masculine*)

der	**Arm, -e**	arm
der	**Bauch, Bäuche**	stomach
der	**Finger**	finger
der	**Fuß, ̈e**	foot
der	**Hals, ̈e**	neck, throat
der	**Kopf, ̈e**	head
der	**Magen, - *or* ̈**	stomach
der	**Mund, ̈er**	mouth
der	**Rücken**	back
der	**Zahn, ̈e**	tooth

ESSENTIAL WORDS (*feminine*)

die	**Bewegung, -en**	movement, motion
die	**Hand, ̈e**	hand
die	**Nase, -n**	nose
die	**Seite, -n**	side

ESSENTIAL WORDS (*neuter*)

das	**Auge, -n**	eye
das	**Bein, -e**	leg
das	**Fleisch**	flesh
das	**Gesicht, -er**	face
das	**Haar, -e**	hair
das	**Ohr, -en**	ear

USEFUL PHRASES

ich habe mir den Arm/das Bein gebrochen I've broken my arm/leg
mein Arm/Bein tut weh my arm/leg hurts
zu Fuß on foot; barfuß gehen to go *or* walk barefoot
von Kopf bis Fuß from head to foot, from top to toe
den Kopf schütteln to shake one's head
mit den Kopf nicken to nod one's head
jdm die Hand geben to shake hands with sb
(mit der Hand) winken to wave
auf etwas zeigen to point to something

IMPORTANT WORDS (masculine)

der	**Atem**	breath
der	**Daumen**	thumb
der	**Körper**	body
der	**Körperteil, -e**	part of the body
der	**Zeigefinger**	forefinger, index finger

IMPORTANT WORDS (feminine)

die	**Lippe, -n**	lip
die	**Schulter, -n**	shoulder
die	**Stimme, -n**	voice
die	**Zunge, -n**	tongue

IMPORTANT WORDS (neuter)

das	**Blut**	blood
das	**Herz, -en**	heart
das	**Knie**	knee

USEFUL PHRASES

sehen to see; hören to hear
fühlen to feel; riechen to smell
tasten to touch; schmecken to taste
sich die Nase putzen to blow one's nose
jdm auf die Schulter klopfen to tap sb on the shoulder
sein Herz klopfte his heart was beating
die linke/rechte Körperseite the left-hand/right-hand side of the body
neben mir at my side
eine leise/laute Stimme haben to have a soft/loud voice
leise/laut sprechen to speak softly/loudly
ich lasse mir die Haare schneiden I'm having my hair cut
auf den Knien on one's knees
stehen to stand; sitzen to sit
sich legen to lie down; knien to kneel (down)
bewegen to move (part of the body)
sich bewegen to move

USEFUL WORDS (masculine)

der	Ell(en)bogen	elbow
der	(Fuß)knöchel	ankle
der	Hintern	bottom
der	Kiefer	jaw
der	Knöchel	knuckle; ankle
der	Knochen	bone
der	Muskel, -n	muscle
der	Nacken	nape of the neck
der	Nagel, ¨	nail
der	Nerv, -en	nerve
der	Schenkel	thigh

USEFUL WORDS (neuter)

das	(Augen)lid, -er	eyelid
das	Blutgefäß, -e	blood vessel
das	Fußgelenk, -e	ankle
das	Gehirn, -e	brain
das	Gelenk, -e	joint
das	Genick, -e	nape of the neck
das	Glied, -er	limb
das	Handgelenk, -e	wrist
das	Kinn, -e	chin
die	Maße (pl)	measurements
das	Rückgrat, -e	spine
das	Skelett, -e	skeleton

USEFUL PHRASES

ich habe mir den Knöchel verstaucht I've sprained my ankle
biegen to bend; strecken to stretch
stürzen to fall; verletzen, verwunden to injure
müde tired
fit fit; unfit unfit
ich ruhe mich aus I'm resting or having a rest
taub deaf; blind blind; stumm dumb
körperbehindert physically handicapped
geistig behindert mentally handicapped

USEFUL WORDS *(feminine)*

die	**Ader, -n**	vein
die	**Arterie, -n**	artery
die	**Augenbraue, -n**	eyebrow
die	**(Augen)wimper, -n**	eyelash
die	**Brust, ⁝e**	breast; chest
die	**Faust, Fäuste**	fist
die	**Ferse, -n**	heel
die	**Figur, -en**	figure
die	**Form, -en**	shape, figure
die	**Fußsohle, -n**	sole of the foot
die	**Gestalt, -en**	figure, form, shape
die	**Geste, -n**	gesture
die	**Haut**	skin
die	**Hüfte, -n**	hip
die	**Kehle, -n**	throat
die	**Leber, -n**	liver
die	**Lunge, -n**	lung
die	**Niere, -n**	kidney
die	**Pupille, -n**	pupil *(of eye)*
die	**Rippe, -n**	rib
die	**Schläfe, -n**	temple
die	**Schlagader, -n**	artery
die	**Stirn, -en**	forehead
die	**Taille, -n**	waist
die	**Wade, -n**	calf *(of leg)*
die	**Wange, -n**	neck
die	**Zehe, -n**	toe
die	**große Zehe, -n -n**	big toe

USEFUL PHRASES

Brustumfang *(m)* bust or chest measurement
Hüftweite *(f)* hip measurement
Taillenweite *(f)* waist measurement

THE SEASONS

der	Frühling	spring
der	Sommer	summer
der	Herbst	autumn
der	Winter	winter

im Frühling/Sommer/Herbst/Winter in spring/summer/autumn/winter

THE MONTHS

Januar	January	Juli	July
Februar	February	August	August
März	March	September	September
April	April	Oktober	October
Mai	May	November	November
Juni	June	Dezember	December

im September etc in September etc
der erste April April Fools' Day
der Erste Mai May Day
der fünfte November (*Tag der Pulververschwörung in England*) Guy Fawkes
   Night

THE DAYS OF THE WEEK

Montag	Monday
Dienstag	Tuesday
Mittwoch	Wednesday
Donnerstag	Thursday
Freitag	Friday
Samstag Sonnabend }	Saturday
Sonntag	Sunday

USEFUL PHRASES

freitags etc on Fridays etc
am Freitag etc on Friday etc
nächsten/letzten Freitag etc next/last Friday etc
am nächsten Freitag etc the following Friday etc

THE CALENDAR

Advent (m) Advent
der Adventskranz Advent wreath
Allerheiligen (nt) All Saints' Day
der Abend vor Allerheiligen Hallowe'en
Allerseelen (nt) All Souls' Day
Aschermittwoch (m) Ash Wednesday
Dreikönigfest (nt) Epiphany, Twelfth Night
Faschingszeit (f) the Fasching festival, carnival time
Fastenzeit (f) Lent
Fastnacht (f) Shrove Tuesday
Heiliger Abend, Heiligabend (m) Christmas Eve
Karfreitag (m) Good Friday
Neujahr (nt) New Year
Neujahrstag (m) New Year's Day
Ostern (nt) Easter
Ostersonntag (m) Easter Sunday
Palmsonntag (m) Palm Sunday
Passahfest (nt) (Feast of the) Passover
Pfingsten (nt) Whitsun
Pfingstmontag (m) Whit Monday
Silvester, Sylvester (nt) New Year's Eve, Hogmanay
Silvesterabend (m) New Year's Eve, Hogmanay
Valentinstag (m) St Valentine's Day
der Valentinsgruß Valentine card
Weihnachten (nt) Christmas
Weihnachtsabend (m) Christmas Eve
Weihnachtstag (m) Christmas Day
zweiter Weihnachtstag (m) Boxing Day
die Weihnachtskarte Christmas card

USEFUL PHRASES

zu Weihnachten/Ostern/Pfingsten at Christmas/Easter/Whitsun

SPECIAL EVENTS

die	**Beerdigung, -en**	funeral, burial
die	**Bescherung, -en**	distribution of Christmas presents
der	**Feiertag, -e**	holiday
das	**Festival, -s**	festival
der	**Festtag, -e**	holiday
das	**Feuerwerk, -e**	firework display
der	**Feuerwerkskörper**	firework
der	**Friedhof, ̈e**	cemetery, graveyard
der	**Geburtstag, -e**	birthday
das	**Geschenk, -e**	present
die	**Heirat, -en**	marriage
der	**Hochzeitstag, -e**	wedding day
die	**Jahreszeit, -en**	season
der	**Kalender**	calendar
das	**Konfetti**	confetti
der	**Wochentag, -e**	weekday
der	**Tanz, ̈e** or **Tanzabend**	dance
die	**Taufe, -n**	christening, baptism
der	**Tod, -e**	death
der	**Werktag, -e**	working day
der	**Zirkus, -se**	circus

USEFUL PHRASES

seinen Geburtstag feiern **to celebrate one's birthday**
der Silvestertanz **New Year's Eve dance**
prosit Neujahr! **happy New Year!**
jdm ein Geschenk machen **to give somebody a present**
ein Feuerwerk abbrennen **to set off fireworks**
ihr dritter Hochzeitstag **their third (wedding) anniversary**
beglückwünschen (zu) **to congratulate (on)**
wünschen **to wish**
(herzlich) willkommen! **you are (very) welcome!**
in Trauer **in mourning**
den Wievielten haben wir heute? **what is today's date?**

SPECIAL EVENTS

die	**Blaskapelle, -n**	brass band
das	**Fest, -e**	fête, feast (day)
die	**Flitterwochen** (pl)	honeymoon (time)
das	**Folksongfestival**	folk music festival
die	**Geburt, -en**	birth
die	**Hochzeit, -en**	wedding
die	**Hochzeitsreise, -n**	honeymoon (journey)
der	**Jahrmarkt, ⁻e**	fair
die	**Kirchweih, -en**	fair
die	**Kirmes, -sen**	funfair
die	**Messe, -n**	(commercial) fair
der	**Namenstag, -e**	saint's day
die	**Party, -s**	party
der	**Ruhestand**	retirement
der	**Rummelplatz, ⁻e**	fairground
die	**Trauung, -en**	wedding ceremony
die	**Verabredung, -en**	date (with sb)
die	**Verlobung, -en**	engagement
das	**Volksfest**	funfair
die	**Zeremonie, -n**	ceremony

USEFUL PHRASES

auf eine or zu einer Hochzeit gehen to go to a wedding
silberne/goldene/diamantene Hochzeit silver/golden/diamond wedding
in den Ruhestand gehen to retire, go into retirement
die Stadt mit Blumen ausschmücken to decorate the town with flowers
die ganze Stadt war beflaggt there were flags out all over town
gute Vorsätze fassen to make good resolutions
beerdigen to bury

ESSENTIAL WORDS (masculine)

der	**Camper**	camper (*person*)
der	**Campingplatz, ⸚e**	camp site
der	**Löffel**	spoon
der	**Rucksack, ⸚e**	backpack, rucksack
der	**Schlafsack, ⸚e**	sleeping bag
der	**Teller**	plate
der	**Urlaub**	holiday(s)
der	**Wohnwagen**	caravan
der	**Zuschlag, ⸚e**	extra charge

ESSENTIAL WORDS (feminine)

die	**Anmeldung, -en**	registration
die	**Camperin**	camper (*person*)
die	**Dusche, -n**	shower
die	**Gabel, -n**	fork
die	**Landkarte, -n**	map
die	**Luft, ⸚e**	air
die	**Nacht, ⸚e**	night
die	**Sache, -n**	thing
die	**Tasse, -n**	cup
die	**Toilette, -n**	toilet
die	**Übernachtung, -en**	overnight stay
die	**Waschmaschine, -n**	washing machine

ESSENTIAL WORDS (neuter)

das	**Camping**	camping
das	**Essen**	food; meal
das	**Glas, ⸚er**	glass
das	**Messer**	knife
das	**(Trink)wasser**	(drinking) water
das	**Zelt, -e**	tent

USEFUL PHRASES

Camping machen **to go camping**
ein Zelt aufbauen *or* aufschlagen **to pitch a tent**
ein Zelt abbauen **to take down a tent**
„Zelten verboten!" **"no camping"**

IMPORTANT + USEFUL WORDS *(masculine)*

der	Aufenthalt, -e	stay
der	Campingkocher	camping stove
der	Dosenöffner	tin-opener
der	Feuerlöscher	fire extinguisher
der	Klappstuhl, ¨e	folding chair
der	Klapptisch, -e	folding table
der	Korkenzieher	corkscrew
der	Liegestuhl, ¨e	deck chair
der	Mülleimer	dustbin
der	Rasierapparat, -e	razor
der	Schatten	shade; shadow
der	Waschraum, -räume	washroom
der	Zeltboden, ¨	ground sheet
der	Zimmernachweis, -e	accommodation office

IMPORTANT + USEFUL WORDS *(feminine)*

die	Büchse, -n	tin, can; box
die	Luftmatratze, -n	lilo, air bed
die	Nachtruhe	lights-out
die	Ruhe	peace; rest
die	Taschenlampe, -n	torch
die	Unterkunft, ¨e	accommodation
die	Veranstaltung, -en	organization
die	Wäsche	washing *(things)*
die	Wäscherei, -en	laundry *(place)*

IMPORTANT + USEFUL WORDS *(neuter)*

das	Campinggas	camping gas
das	Fahrzeug, -e	vehicle
das	Geschirr	dishes, crockery; pots and pans
das	Lagerfeuer	campfire
das	Streichholz, ¨er	match
das	Waschpulver	washing powder, detergent
das	Wohnmobil, -e	camper, motor caravan

ESSENTIAL WORDS (masculine)

der	Arbeiter	worker, labourer
	Arbeitslose(r), -n	unemployed man/woman
der	Arzt, ̈-e	doctor
der	Briefträger	postman
der	Chef, -s	boss, head
der	Geschäftsmann, -leute	businessman
der	Job, -s	(spare time) job
der	Koch, ̈-e	cook
der	Krankenpfleger	nurse
der	Last(kraft)wagenfahrer;	lorry driver
	der LKW-Fahrer	
der	Lehrer	teacher
der	Polizist, -en	policeman
der	Taxifahrer	taxi driver
der	Techniker	technician
der	Teilzeitjob, -s	part-time job
der	Zahnarzt, ̈-e	dentist

ESSENTIAL WORDS (feminine)

die	Arbeit, -en	work; job
die	Arbeiterin	worker
die	Ärztin	doctor
die	Bank, -en	bank
die	Bezahlung, -en	payment
die	Chefin	boss
die	Empfangsdame, -n	receptionist
die	Fabrik, -en	factory
die	Geschäftsfrau, -en	businesswoman
die	Geschäftsreise, -n	business trip
die	Industrie, -n	industry
die	Köchin	cook
die	Krankenschwester, -n	nurse
die	Lehrerin	teacher
die	Polizistin	policewoman
die	Zahnärztin	dentist

ESSENTIAL WORDS *(neuter)*

das **Büro, -s**   office
das **Geschäft, -e**   business, trade; shop
das **Job-Center, -s**   job centre

USEFUL PHRASES

arbeiten **to work**; bei X arbeiten **to work at X's**
interessant **interesting**; langweilig **boring**
mit der Arbeit anfangen, zu arbeiten beginnen **to start work,
  get down to work**
berufstätig sein **to be employed**
arbeitslos sein **to be out of work, be unemployed**
arbeitslos werden **to be made redundant**
Arbeitslosengeld beziehen **to be on the dole**
seine Stelle verlieren **to lose one's job**
entlassen **to dismiss**
entlassen werden **to be sacked, get the sack**
jobben **to do odd jobs**
eine Stelle suchen **to look for a job**
„Stellenangebote" **"situations vacant"**
fest **permanent**; vorübergehend **temporary**
ganztags **full-time**; halbtags **part-time**
sich um eine Stelle bewerben **to apply for a job**
eine Stelle antreten **to start a new job**
verdienen **to earn**
500 Pfund in der Woche verdienen **to earn £500 per week**
sparen für *(+ acc)* **to save up for**
was sind Sie von Beruf? **what is your job?**
ich bin Elektriker (von Beruf) **I am an electrician (to trade)**
ehrgeizig **ambitious**
selbstständig **self-employed**
ich möchte Sekretärin werden **I'd like to be a secretary**
sein eigenes Geschäft haben **to have one's own shop** *or* **business**
eine Geschäftsreise machen **to go away on business**
streiken **to strike, be on strike**

IMPORTANT WORDS (masculine)

Angestellte(r), -n	employee
der Apotheker	chemist
der Arbeitgeber	employer
der Arbeitslohn, ⁻e	wages, pay
der Arbeitnehmer	employee
der Architekt, -en	architect
der Arzthelfer	doctor's receptionist
der Astronaut, -en	astronaut
der Bankkaufmann, -leute	bank clerk
der Bäcker	baker
Beamte(r), -n	official
der Beruf, -e	profession, occupation
der Betrieb, -e	firm, concern
der Bibliothekar, -e	librarian
Büroangestellte(r), -n	office worker, clerk
der Elektriker	electrician
der Feuerwehrmann, -männer	fireman
der Fotograf, -en	photographer
der Friseur, -e	hairdresser
der Geschäftsführer	executive; manager
der Informatiker	computer scientist
der Ingenieur, -e	engineer
der Journalist, -en	journalist
der Kfz-Mechaniker	motor mechanic
der Lehrling, -e	apprentice, trainee
der Lohn, ⁻e	wages, pay
der Maler	painter
der Pilot, -en	pilot
der Politiker	politician
der Präsident, -en	president
der Premierminister	prime minister, premier
der Priester	priest
der Reporter	reporter
der Sekretär, -e	secretary
der Star, -s	star
der Tierarzt, ⁻e	veterinary surgeon, vet
der Verkäufer	salesman, shop assistant
der Webdesigner	Web designer

IMPORTANT WORDS (feminine)

die	Arbeitnehmerin	employee
die	Architektin	architect
die	Arzthelferin	doctor's receptionist
die	Astronautin	astronaut
die	Bäckerin	baker
die	Bankkauffrau, -en	bank clerk
die	Beamtin	official
die	Berufsberatung	careers or vocational guidance
die	Bewerbung	application
die	Bibliothekarin	librarian
die	Firma, Firmen	firm, company
die	Friseuse, -n	hairdresser
die	Geschäftsführerin	executive; manageress
die	Gesellschaft, -en	company
die	Informatikerin	computer scientist
die	Journalistin	journalist
die	Kfz-Mechanikerin	motor mechanic
die	Lehrzeit, -en	apprenticeship
die	Politikerin	politician
die	Putzfrau, -en	cleaner, cleaning woman
die	Sekretärin	secretary
die	Stelle, -n	job, post
die	Tagesmutter, ⸚	child minder
die	Tierärztin	veterinary surgeon, vet
die	Verkäuferin	salesgirl, shop assistant
die	Webdesignerin	Web designer
die	Zukunft	future

IMPORTANT WORDS (neuter)

das	Einkommen	income
das	Gehalt, ⸚er	salary
das	Handwerk, -e	trade; craft
das	Kindermädchen	nanny
das	Model, -s	model

USEFUL WORDS (*masculine*)

	Abgeordnete(r), -n	M.P., member of parliament
der	Augenoptiker	optician
der	Autor, -en	author
der	Bauunternehmer	builder, building contractor
der	Bergarbeiter	miner
der	Betriebsleiter	managing director
der	Chirurg, -en	surgeon
der	Dichter	poet
der	Dolmetscher	interpreter
der	Florist, -en	florist
der	Forscher	researcher
der	Gewerkschaftler	trade unionist
der	Handel	commerce
der	Hausmeister	caretaker; janitor
der	Hotelfachmann, -leute	hotel manager
der	Kameramann, -männer	cameraman
der	Klempner	plumber
der	König, -e	king
der	Künstler	artist
der	Matrose, -n	sailor
der	Modeschöpfer	fashion designer
der	Mönch, -e	monk
der	Pfarrer	minister, clergyman
der	Produzent, -en	manufacturer; (film) producer
der	Rechtsanwalt, ̈-e	lawyer, solicitor
der	Redakteur, -e	editor
der	Schneider	tailor
der	Schriftsteller	writer
der	Soldat, -en	soldier
der	Tischler	joiner, carpenter
der	Verleger	publisher
der	Vertreter	representative, rep
	Vorsitzende(r), -n	chairman/-woman
der	Winzer	wine grower, vineyard owner
der	Wirtschaftsprüfer	chartered accountant
der	Wissenschaftler	scientist

USEFUL WORDS *(feminine)*

die	Absicht, -en	intention, aim
die	Augenoptikerin	optician
die	Ausbildung	training, education
die	Autorin	author
die	Chirurgin	surgeon
die	Dichterin	poet
die	Dolmetscherin	interpreter
die	Floristin	florist
die	Forscherin	researcher
die	Gewerkschaft, -en	trade union
die	Hotelfachfrau, -en	hotel manageress
die	Jobvermittlung, -en	employment agency
die	Kamerafrau, -en	camerawoman
die	Königin	queen
die	Künstlerin	artist
die	Laufbahn, -en	career
die	Leiterin	leader, manager
die	Lohnerhöhung, -en	wage increase
die	Modeschöpferin	fashion designer
die	Nonne, -n	nun
die	Platzanweiserin	usherette
die	Rechtsanwältin	lawyer, solicitor
die	Redakteurin	editor
die	Schneiderin	dressmaker
die	Schriftstellerin	writer
die	Soldatin	soldier
die	Sprechstundenhilfe, -n	(medical) receptionist
die	Stenotypistin	shorthand typist
die	Stewardess, -en	flight attendant
die	Verwaltung, -en	administration
die	Wissenschaftlerin	scientist

ESSENTIAL WORDS (masculine)

der (Auto)fahrer	motorist, driver
der Diesel	diesel (oil)
der Führerschein, -e	driving licence
der Kilometer	kilometre
der Koffer	suitcase
der Lastkraftwagen (LKW)	lorry, truck
der Lastwagenfahrer	lorry driver
der Liter	litre
der Parkplatz, ̈e	parking space; car park
der Passagier, -e	passenger
der Personenkraftwagen (PKW)	private car
der Polizist, -en	policeman
der Rasthof, ̈e	service station
der Rastplatz, ̈e	lay-by
der Reifen	tyre
der Reifendruck	tyre pressure
der (Sport)wagen	(sports) car
der Weg, -e	road, way
der Wohnwagen	caravan

ESSENTIAL WORDS (neuter)

das Auto, -s	car
das Benzin, -e	petrol
das Dieselöl	diesel (oil)
das Gepäck	luggage
das Mietauto, -s	hired car
das Normalbenzin	2-star (petrol)
das Öl, -e	oil
das Parkhaus, -häuser	(covered) multistorey car park
das Parken	parking
das Rad, ̈er	wheel
das Selbsttanken	self-service petrol
das Straßenschild, -er	road sign
das Super	4-star (petrol)
das Wasser	water

ESSENTIAL WORDS (feminine)

die	Achtung	attention
die	Ampel, -n	traffic lights
die	Ausfahrt, -en	exit; drive; slip road
die	Autobahn, -en	motorway
die	(Auto)fahrerin	motorist, driver
die	Bahn, -en	road, way; lane
die	Batterie, -n	battery
die	Ecke, -n	corner
die	Einbahnstraße, -n	one-way street
die	Fahrt, -en	journey; trip; drive
die	Garage, -n	garage
die	Hauptstraße, -n	main road, main street
die	grüne Versicherungskarte,-n, -n	green card
die	Landkarte, -n	map
die	Maschine, -n	engine
die	Meile, -n	mile
die	Polizei	police
die	Polizistin	policewoman
die	Raststätte, -n	service area
die	Reise, -n	journey
die	Reparatur, -en	repair; repairing
die	(Reparatur)werkstatt, ⁀en	garage, workshop
die	Richtung, -en	direction
die	Selbstbedienung (SB)	self-service
die	Straße, -n	street, road
die	Straßenkarte, -n	road map, plan
die	Straßenverkehrsordnung	Highway Code
die	Tankstelle, -n	petrol station, filling station, service station
die	Umleitung, -en	diversion
die	Verkehrsampel, -n	traffic lights
die	Vorfahrt	right of way
die	Vorsicht	caution, care
die	Warnung, -en	warning
die	Werkstatt, ⁀en	garage, workshop

IMPORTANT WORDS (masculine)

der	Abstand, ̈e	distance
der	Blinker	indicator
der	Chauffeur, -e	chauffeur
der	Dachgepäckträger	roof rack
der	Fahrlehrer	driving instructor
der	Fahrschüler	learner driver
der	Fußgänger	pedestrian
der	Gang, ̈e	gear
der	Kofferraum, -räume	boot
der	Mechaniker	mechanic; engineer
der	Motorschaden, -schäden	engine trouble
der	Parkschein, -e	parking permit
der	Rückspiegel	rear-view or driving mirror
der	Scheinwerfer	headlight, headlamp
der	Sicherheitsgurt, -e	seat belt
der	Stau, -e	(traffic) jam
der	Tramper	hitch-hiker
der	Umweg, -e	detour
der	Unfall, ̈e	accident
der	Verkehr	traffic
der	Verkehrspolizist, -en	traffic warden
der	Verkehrsunfall, ̈e	road accident
	Verletzte(r), -n	casualty
der	Zusammenstoß, ̈e	collision, crash

IMPORTANT WORDS (neuter)

das	Autobahndreieck, -e	motorway junction
das	Autobahnkreuz, -e	motorway intersection
das	Fahrzeug, -e	vehicle
das	Firmenauto, -s	company car
das	Navigationssystem, -e	(satellite) navigation system
das	Parkverbot, -e	parking ban
das	Reserverad, ̈er	spare wheel
das	Trampen	hitch-hiking
das	Wohngebiet, -e	built-up area

IMPORTANT WORDS *(feminine)*

die **Autoschlange, -n**	line of cars
die **Autowäsche, -n**	car wash
die **Bremse, -n**	brake
die **Fahrlehrerin**	driving instructress
die **Fahrprüfung, -en**	driving test
die **Fahrschule, -n**	driving school
die **Fahrschülerin**	learner driver
die **Fahrstunde, -n**	driving lesson
die **Gebühr, -en**	toll
die **Gefahr, -en**	danger, risk
die **Geldstrafe, -n**	fine
die **Geschwindigkeit, -en**	speed
die **Grenze, -n**	border, frontier
die **Hauptverkehrszeit, -en**	rush hour
die **Kreuzung, -en**	crossroads
die **Kurve, -n**	bend, corner
die **Notbremsung, -en**	emergency stop
die **Panne, -n**	breakdown
die **Parkuhr, -en**	parking meter
die **Querstraße, -n**	junction, intersection
die **Reifenpanne, -n**	puncture
die **(Reise)route, -n**	route, itinerary
die **Ringstraße, -n**	ring road
die **Tiefgarage, -n**	underground garage
die **Verkehrspolizistin**	traffic warden
die **Versicherung, -en**	insurance
die **Windschutzscheibe, -n**	windscreen

USEFUL PHRASES

fahren to drive; abfahren to leave, set off
einsteigen to get in; aussteigen to get out
sich anschnallen to put on one's seat belt
(voll) tanken to fill up (with petrol)
reisen to travel
hinten in the back; vorn(e) in the front

USEFUL WORDS *(masculine)*

der **Abschleppdienst**	breakdown service
der **Abschleppwagen**	breakdown van
der **Anhänger**	trailer
der **Anlasser**	starter
der **Durchgangsverkehr**	through traffic
der **Fußgängerüberweg, -e**	pedestrian crossing
der **Katalysator, -en**	catalytic converter
der **Kreisverkehr, -e**	roundabout
der **Leerlauf**	neutral (gear)
der **Scheibenwischer**	windscreen wiper
der **Strafzettel**	(parking) ticket
der **Tachometer**	speedometer
der **Verkehrsrowdy, -s**	road hog
der **Wagenheber**	jack

USEFUL WORDS *(neuter)*

das **Armaturenbrett, -er**	dashboard
das **Ersatzreifen**	spare tyre
das **Ersatzteil, -e**	spare part
das **Getriebe**	gearbox
das **Kat-Auto, -s**	car with a catalytic converter
das **polizeiliche Kennzeichen**	registration number
das **Lenkrad, -̈er**	steering wheel
das **Nummernschild, -er**	number plate
das **Steuerrad, -̈er**	steering wheel
das **Verdeck, -e**	hood
das **Verkehrsdelikt, -e**	traffic offence
das **Warndreieck, -e**	warning triangle

USEFUL PHRASES

gute Reise! have a good trip!
bremsen to brake; schalten to change gear
hupen to sound or toot the horn
überholen to overtake; sich einordnen to get into lane
abbiegen to turn off; halten to stop
abstellen to park, to switch off; abschleppen to tow away
parken to park; abschließen to lock; ankommen to arrive

USEFUL WORDS *(feminine)*

die	**Abzweigung, -en**	junction
die	**Auffahrt, -en**	slip road
die	**Autovermietung, -en**	car hire
die	**Beleuchtung, -en**	lights *(pl)*
die	**Biegung, -en**	bend, curve
die	**Gasse, -n**	alley, lane, back street
die	**Geschwindigkeits-**	speed limit, speed
	begrenzung, -en	restriction
die	**Hupe, -n**	horn, hooter
die	**Karosserie, -n**	bodywork, body
die	**Kupplung, -en**	clutch
die	**Marke, -n**	make *(of car)*
die	**(Motor)haube, -n**	bonnet
die	**Politesse, -n**	traffic warden
die	**Stoßstange, -n**	bumper
die	**(Versicherungs)police, -n**	insurance policy

USEFUL PHRASES

schnell **fast**; langsam **slowly**
gefährlich **dangerous**; kaputt **broken, done**
sperren **to block**; prüfen **to check**
Abstand halten **to keep one's distance**
in ein Auto fahren **to bump into a car**
das Auto reparieren lassen **to have the car repaired**
100 Kilometer in der Stunde machen **to do 100 kilometres an hour**
beschleunigen, Gas geben **to accelerate**
die Ampel überfahren **to go through the lights at red**
mir ist das Benzin ausgegangen **I've run out of petrol**
verbleit **leaded**; unverbleit, bleifrei **unleaded**
sich verfahren **to get lost, take the wrong road**
sich zurechtfinden **to find one's way**
trampen, per Anhalter fahren **to hitch-hike**
„Anlieger frei" **"residents only"**
„Parken verboten" **"no parking"**; „freihalten" **"keep clear"**
„Vorfahrt achten" **"give way"**

ESSENTIAL WORDS (masculine)

der	**Anorak, -s**	anorak
der	**Badeanzug, ⸚e**	swimming or bathing costume
der	**Gürtel**	belt
der	**Handschuh, -e**	glove
der	**Kleiderschrank, ⸚e**	wardrobe
der	**Knopf, ⸚e**	button
der	**Mantel, ⸚e**	coat, overcoat
der	**Pullover; der Pulli, -s**	pullover, jumper, jersey
der	**Pyjama, -s**	(pair of) pyjamas
der	**Regenmantel, ⸚**	raincoat
der	**Rock, ⸚e**	skirt
der	**Schlips, -e**	tie
der	**Schuh, -e**	shoe
der	**(Spazier)stock, ⸚e**	walking stick
der	**Umkleideraum, -räume**	changing room

USEFUL PHRASES

ich ziehe mich an I get dressed, I put on my clothes
ich ziehe mich aus I get undressed, I take off my clothes
ich ziehe mich um I get changed, I change my clothes
tragen to wear
Hosen/einen Mantel tragen to wear trousers/a coat
seine Schuhe/seinen Mantel anziehen to put on one's shoes/coat
seine Schuhe/seinen Mantel ausziehen to take off one's shoes/coat
einen Hut tragen to wear a hat
sich (dat) den Hut aufsetzen to put on one's hat
den Hut abnehmen to take off one's hat
darf ich dieses Kleid anprobieren? may I try on this dress?
das steht Ihnen (gut) that suits you
passen to fit; groß big; klein small
das passt mir nicht that doesn't fit me; passend matching
waschen to wash; bügeln to iron
chemisch reinigen to dryclean

ESSENTIAL WORDS (feminine)

die	Badehose, -n	swimming or bathing trunks
die	Bluse, -n	blouse
die	Brille, -n	(pair of) glasses
die	Größe, -n	size
die	Handtasche, -n	handbag
die	Hose, -n	(pair of) trousers
die	Jacke, -n	jacket
die	Jeans (pl)	jeans
die	Kleidung	clothing
die	Krawatte, -n	tie
die	Lederhose, -n	(pair of) leather shorts or trousers
die	Mode, -n	fashion
die	Sandale, -n	sandal
die	Socke, -n	sock
die	Tasche, -n	pocket; bag

ESSENTIAL WORDS (neuter)

das	Abendkleid, -er	evening dress (woman's)
das	Band, ‑er	ribbon
das	Hemd, -en	shirt
das	Kleid, -er	dress
die	Kleider (pl)	clothes, clothing
das	Nachthemd, -en	nightdress; nightshirt
das	Taschentuch, ‑er	handkerchief
das	T-Shirt, -s	T-shirt, tee-shirt

USEFUL PHRASES

bunt coloured; kariert checked; gestreift striped
in Mode in fashion
modisch fashionable; unmodisch out of fashion
altmodisch old-fashioned; sehr schick very smart
Brustumfang (m) bust or chest measurement
Hüftweite (f) hip measurement
Kragenweite (f) collar size; Schuhgröße (f) shoe size
Taillenweite (f) waist measurement

IMPORTANT WORDS (masculine)

der	Anzug, ̈e	suit
der	BH, -s (Büstenhalter)	bra
der	Hausschuh, -e	slipper
der	Hut, ̈e	hat
der	Overall, -s	(set of) overalls
der	Schal, -e or -s	scarf
der	Schlafanzug, ̈e	(pair of) pyjamas
der	Schleier	veil
der	Stiefel	boot
der	Strumpf, ̈e	stocking, (long) sock
der	Trainingsanzug, ̈e	tracksuit
der	Turban, -e	turban
die	Turnschuhe (pl)	trainers, training shoes
der	Unterrock, ̈e	underskirt, petticoat

IMPORTANT WORDS (feminine)

die	Fliege, -n	bow tie
die	Freizeitkleidung	casual clothes
die	Herrenkonfektion	menswear
die	Modenschau, -en	fashion show
die	Mütze, -n	cap
die	Schultertasche, -n	shoulder bag
die	Strumpfhose, -n	(pair of) tights
die	Uniform, -en	uniform
die	Unterhose, -n	(under)pants (pl)
die	Unterwäsche	underwear
die	Wäsche, -n	washing; (under)clothes

IMPORTANT WORDS (neuter)

das	Blouson, -s	bomber jacket
das	Jackett, -s or -e	jacket
das	Kostüm, -e	(lady's) suit
die	Shorts (pl)	shorts
das	Sweatshirt, -s	sweatshirt
das	Unterhemd, -en	vest

USEFUL WORDS (masculine)

der Ärmel	sleeve
der Gesellschaftsanzug, ⸚e	evening dress (man's)
der Hosenanzug, ⸚e	trouser suit
der Hosenrock, ⸚e	culottes
der Hosenträger	braces (pl)
der Jogginganzug, ⸚e	jogging suit
der Kragen	collar
die Lumpen (pl)	rags
der Morgenrock, ⸚e	dressing gown
der Reißverschluss, ⸚e	zip
der Rollkragen	polo neck
der Schnürsenkel	shoelace
der Smoking, -s	dinner jacket

USEFUL WORDS (feminine)

die Falte, -n	pleat
die Kappe, -n	cap, hood
die Kragenweite, -n	collar size
die Latzhose, -n	dungarees
die Markenkleidung	branded clothes (pl)
die Melone, -n	bowler hat
die Schürze, -n	apron
die Strickjacke, -n	cardigan
die Tracht, -en	costume, dress
die Weste, -n	waistcoat
die Wolljacke, -n	cardigan

USEFUL WORDS (neuter)

das Hochzeitskleid, -er	wedding dress
das Kopftuch, ⸚er	headscarf, headsquare
das Zubehör	accessories (pl)

USEFUL PHRASES

sich verkleiden to disguise oneself; maskiert masked
maßgeschneidert made to measure
von der Stange off the peg

beige	beige, fawn
blau	blue
braun	brown
gelb	yellow
golden	golden
grau	grey
grün	green
lila	purple
orange	orange
pink	shocking pink
rehbraun	fawn
rosa	pink
rot	red
schwarz	black
silbern	silver
veilchenblau	violet
violett	violet, purple
weiß	white
dunkelblau	dark blue
hellblau	light blue, pale blue
bläulich	bluish
himmelblau	sky blue
königsblau	royal blue
marineblau	navy blue

USEFUL PHRASES
das Blau steht ihr blue suits her
etwas blau anstreichen to paint something blue
die Farbe wechseln to change colour
bunte/dunkle Farben bright/dark colours
das Farbfernsehen colour television

SOME COLOURFUL PHRASES

was für eine Farbe hat es? **what colour is it?**
blau vor Kälte **blue with cold**
eine Fahrt ins Blaue **a mystery tour**
ein blaues Auge **a black eye**
sie hat blaue Augen **she has blue eyes**
braun werden **to go *or* turn brown (*people, leaves*)**
gelb vor Neid **green with envy**
grün und blau **black and blue**
die grüne Versicherungskarte **green card (*for motor insurance*)**
die Grünen **the Green party**
Rotkäppchen **Little Red Riding Hood**
in den roten Zahlen **in the red, in debt**
in den schwarzen Zahlen **in the black**
ein Schwarzer **a black man**
eine Schwarze **a black woman**
ein schwarzes Brett **a notice board**
ein Weißer **a white man**
eine Weiße **a white woman**
das Weiße Haus **the White House**
schneeweiß **as white as snow**
leichenblass **as white as a sheet**

ESSENTIAL + IMPORTANT WORDS *(masculine)*

der	**Bildschirm, -e**	monitor, screen
der	**Computer**	computer
der	**Cursor**	cursor
der	**Drucker**	printer
der	**Monitor, -e**	monitor
der	**PC, -s**	PC, personal computer
der	**Programmierer**	(computer) programmer
der	**Speicher**	memory
der	**Virus, Viren**	virus

ESSENTIAL + IMPORTANT WORDS *(feminine)*

die	**CD-ROM, -s**	CD-ROM
die	**Datei, -en**	file
die	**Diskette, -n**	disk; floppy disk
die	**E-Mail, -s**	e-mail
die	**Festplatte, -n**	hard disk
die	**Hardware**	hardware
die	**Maus, Mäuse**	mouse
die	**Sicherheitskopie, -n**	backup (copy)
die	**Software**	software
die	**Tastatur, -en**	keyboard
die	**Taste, -n**	key

ESSENTIAL + IMPORTANT WORDS *(neuter)*

das	**Betriebssystem, -e**	operating system
das	**Breitband**	broadband
die	**Daten** *(pl)*	data
das	**Fenster**	window
das	**Internet**	Internet
das	**Laufwerk, -e**	drive
das	**Menü, -s**	menu
das	**Modem, -s**	modem
das	**Passwort, -wörter**	password
das	**Popup-Menü, -s**	pop-up menu
das	**Programm, -e**	program

USEFUL WORDS *(masculine)*

der	**Ausdruck, -e**	printout
der	**Benutzer**	user
der	**Browser**	browser
der	**Chip, -s**	chip
der	**Hacker**	hacker
der	**Heimcomputer**	home computer
der	**Informatiker**	computer scientist
der	**Joystick, -s**	joystick
der	**Laserdrucker**	laser printer
der	**Ordner**	folder
der	**Papierkorb, ⁓e**	trash, recycle bin
der	**Programmierer**	(computer) programmer
der	**Provider**	provider
der	**Rechner**	computer; calculator
der	**Schrägstrich, -e**	slash
der	**Seitenwechsel**	page break
der	**Server**	server
der	**Spamfilter**	spam filter
der	**Tintenstrahldrucker**	ink-jet (printer)
der	**Zeilenabstand, ⁓e**	line spacing

USEFUL WORDS *(feminine)*

die	**Anwendung, -en**	application
die	**Datenbank, -en**	database
die	**Eingabetaste, -n**	enter key
die	**E-Mail-Adresse, -n**	e-mail address
die	**Funktion, -en**	function
die	**Hilfefunktion, -en**	help function
die	**Homepage, -s**	homepage

USEFUL PHRASES

spielen to play; sich amüsieren to have fun
ein Programm schreiben to write a program
den Computer programmieren to program the computer
den Cursor bewegen to move the cursor; klicken to click
bearbeiten to edit; einfügen to insert; to paste
formatieren to format; kopieren to copy; löschen to delete

USEFUL WORDS *(feminine continued)*

die **Informatik**	computer science, computing
die **Internetauktion, -en**	Internet auction
die **Leertaste, -n**	space bar
die **Löschtaste, -n**	delete key
die **Mausmatte, -n**	mouse pad
die **Rechtschreibprüfung, -en**	spellchecker
die **Schaltfläche, -n**	button
die **Schnittstelle, -n**	interface
die **Schriftart, -en**	font
die **Sicherungskopie, -n**	back-up (copy)
die **Suchmaschine, -n**	search engine
die **Tabellenkalkulation, -en**	spreadsheet (program)
die **Textverarbeitung, -en**	word processor
die **Webadresse, -n**	Web address
die **Webseite, -n**	Web page

USEFUL WORDS *(neuter)*

das **Bildschirmgerät, -e**	VDU, visual display unit
das **CD-ROM-Laufwerk, -e**	CD-ROM drive
das **Computerspiel, -e**	computer game
das **Diskettenlaufwerk, -e**	disk drive
das **Dokument, -e**	document
das **DVD-Laufwerk, -e**	DVD drive
das **Interface, -s**	interface
das **Notebook, -s**	notebook (computer)
das **Programmieren**	(computer) programming
das **RAM**	RAM *(random access memory)*
das **ROM**	ROM *(read only memory)*
das **Symbol, -e**	icon
das **Virensuchprogramm, -e**	virus checker
das **Zeichen**	character

USEFUL PHRASES

die Daten speichern **to store the data**; die Daten sichern **to save the data**
im Internet surfen **to surf the Internet**; ausdrucken **to print out**; mailen **to e-mail**
elektronisch **electronic**; fett **bold**; kursiv **italic**; mager **roman**; tragbar **portable**
linksbündig **left adjusted**; rechtsbündig **right adjusted**

COUNTRIES

All countries are neuter unless marked otherwise. Where an article is shown, the noun is used with the article.

	Afrika	Africa
	Asien	Asia
	Australien	Australia
	Belgien	Belgium
	Brasilien	Brazil
	Bulgarien	Bulgaria
die	Bundesrepublik Deutschland (BRD)	Germany
	China	China
	Dänemark	Denmark
	Deutschland	Germany
	England	England
	Europa	Europe
die	Europäische Union (EU)	the European Union (EU)
	Finnland	Finland
	Frankreich	France
	Großbritannien	Great Britain
	Griechenland	Greece
	Holland	Holland
	Indien	India
der	Irak	Iraq
der	Iran	Iran
	Irland	Ireland
	Italien	Italy
	Japan	Japan
	Kanada	Canada
	Korea	Korea
	Luxemburg	Luxembourg
	Mexiko	Mexico
	Neuseeland	New Zealand
die	Niederlande (pl)	the Netherlands
	Nordirland	Northern Ireland
	Norwegen	Norway
	Österreich	Austria

COUNTRIES (continued)

	Pakistan	Pakistan
	Polen	Poland
	Portugal	Portugal
	Rumänien	Romania
	Russland	Russia
	Saudi-Arabien	Saudi Arabia
	Schottland	Scotland
	Schweden	Sweden
die	Schweiz	Switzerland
	Skandinavien	Scandinavia
	Spanien	Spain
	Südafrika	South Africa
	Südamerika	South America
die	Tschechische Republik	the Czech Republic
die	Türkei	Turkey
	Ungarn	Hungary
das	Vereinigte Königreich	the United Kingdom
die	Vereinigten Staaten	the United States
	(mpl) (von Amerika)	(of America)
	Vietnam	Vietnam
	Wales	Wales

USEFUL PHRASES

in die Niederlande/in die Schweiz fahren to go to the Netherlands/
    to Switzerland
nach Deutschland fahren to go to Germany
ein Land, (pl) Länder country
die Entwicklungsländer (pl) developing countries
ins Ausland fahren or gehen to go or travel abroad
im Ausland sein to be abroad
ein Ausländer, eine Ausländerin a foreigner
die Hauptstadt capital
ich bin in Deutschland geboren I was born in Germany

NATIONALITIES *(masculine)*

ein	**Afrikaner**	an African
ein	**Amerikaner**	an American
ein	**Araber**	an Arab
ein	**Asiat, -en**	an Asian
ein	**Australier**	an Australian
ein	**Belgier**	a Belgian
ein	**Brasilianer**	a Brazilian
ein	**Brite, -n**	a Briton (*pl* the British)
ein	**Chinese, -n**	a Chinese
ein	**Däne, -n**	a Dane
ein	**Deutscher, -n**	a German
ein	**Engländer**	an Englishman
ein	**Europäer**	a European
ein	**Finne, -n**	a Finn
ein	**Franzose, -n**	a Frenchman
ein	**Grieche, -n**	a Greek
ein	**Holländer**	a Dutchman
ein	**Inder**	an Indian
ein	**Iraker**	an Iraqi
ein	**Iraner**	an Iranian
ein	**Ire**	an Irishman
ein	**Italiener**	an Italian
ein	**Japaner**	a Japanese
ein	**Kanadier**	a Canadian
ein	**Luxemburger**	a native of Luxemburg
ein	**Mexikaner**	a Mexican
ein	**Neuseeländer**	a New Zealander
ein	**Niederländer**	a Dutchman
ein	**Norweger**	a Norwegian
ein	**Österreicher**	an Austrian
ein	**Pole, -n**	a Pole
ein	**Portugiese, -n**	a Portuguese
ein	**Rumäne, -n**	a Romanian
ein	**Russe, -n**	a Russian
ein	**Schotte, -n**	a Scotsman, a Scot
ein	**Schwede, -n**	a Swede
ein	**Schweizer**	a Swiss
ein	**Spanier**	a Spaniard

NATIONALITIES *(masculine continued)*

ein	**Türke, -n**	a Turk
ein	**Ungar, -n**	a Hungarian
ein	**Vietnamese, -n**	a Vietnamese
ein	**Waliser**	a Welshman

The forms given above and on the following two pages are the noun forms. The corresponding adjectives begin with a small letter and end in -isch.

Most can be formed by changing -er(in) or -ier(in) to -isch.

The main exceptions are as follows: **deutsch** (German), **englisch** (English), **französisch** (French), **schweizerisch** (Swiss).

NATIONALITIES *(feminine)*

eine	**Afrikanerin**	an African (girl or woman)
eine	**Amerikanerin**	an American (girl or woman)
eine	**Araberin**	an Arabian (girl or woman)
eine	**Asiatin**	an Asian (girl or woman)
eine	**Australierin**	an Australian (girl or woman)
eine	**Belgierin**	a Belgian (girl or woman)
eine	**Brasilianerin**	a Brazilian (girl or woman)
eine	**Britin**	a Briton, a British girl or woman
eine	**Chinesin**	a Chinese (girl or woman)
eine	**Dänin**	a Dane, a Danish girl or woman
eine	**Deutsche**	a German (girl or woman)
eine	**Engländerin**	an Englishwoman, an English girl
eine	**Europäerin**	a European (girl or woman)
eine	**Finnin**	a Finn, a Finnish girl or woman
eine	**Französin**	a Frenchwoman, a French girl
eine	**Griechin**	a Greek, a Greek girl or woman
eine	**Holländerin**	a Dutchwoman, a Dutch girl
eine	**Inderin**	an Indian (girl or woman)
eine	**Irakerin**	an Iraqi (girl or woman)
eine	**Iranerin**	an Iranian (girl or woman)
eine	**Irin**	an Irishwoman, an Irish girl
eine	**Italienerin**	an Italian (girl or woman)

NATIONALITIES *(feminine continued)*

eine **Japanerin**	a Japanese (girl *or* woman)
eine **Kanadierin**	a Canadian (girl *or* woman)
eine **Luxemburgerin**	a native of Luxemburg
eine **Mexikanerin**	a Mexican (girl *or* woman)
eine **Neuseeländerin**	a New Zealander, a New Zealand girl *or* woman
eine **Niederländerin**	a Dutchwoman, a Dutch girl
eine **Norwegerin**	a Norwegian (girl *or* woman)
eine **Österreicherin**	an Austrian (girl *or* woman)
eine **Polin**	a Pole, a Polish girl *or* woman
eine **Portugiesin**	a Portuguese (girl *or* woman)
eine **Rumänin**	a Rumanian (girl *or* woman)
eine **Russin**	a Russian (girl *or* woman)
eine **Schottin**	a Scotswoman, a Scots girl
eine **Schwedin**	a Swede, a Swedish girl *or* woman
eine **Schweizerin**	a Swiss girl *or* woman
eine **Spanierin**	a Spaniard, a Spanish girl *or* woman
eine **Türkin**	a Turkish girl *or* woman
eine **Ungarin**	a Hungarian (girl *or* woman)
eine **Vietnamesin**	a Vietnamese (girl *or* woman)
eine **Waliserin**	a Welshwoman, a Welsh girl

USEFUL PHRASES

die Staatsangehörigkeit **nationality**
die Religion **religion**
die Muttersprache **native language**

ESSENTIAL WORDS (masculine)

der	Bauernhof, ¨-e	farmyard, farm
der	Baum, Bäume	tree
der	Berg, -e	mountain, hill
der	Fluss, ¨-e	river
der	Gasthof, ¨-e	inn
der	Grund	ground
der	Hügel	hill
der	Lärm	noise
der	Markt, ¨-e	market
der	See, -n	lake
der	Stein, -e	stone, rock
der	Stock, ¨-e	cane, stick
der	Turm, ¨-e	tower; (church) steeple
der	Wald, ¨-er	wood, forest

ESSENTIAL WORDS (neuter)

das	Dorf, ¨-er	village
das	Feld, -er	field
das	Gasthaus, -häuser	inn
das	Land, ¨-er	land; country
das	Picknick, -e or -s	picnic
das	Schloss, ¨-er	castle
das	Tal, ¨-er	valley
das	Wirtshaus, -häuser	inn

USEFUL PHRASES

aufs Land gehen to go into the country
auf dem Lande wohnen to live in the country
auf dem Bauernhof on the farm
ein Picknick machen to go for a picnic
im Freien in the open air

ESSENTIAL WORDS *(feminine)*

die **Blume, -n**	flower
die **Brücke, -n**	bridge
die **Burg, -en**	castle
die **Höhle, -n**	cave, hole
die **Jugendherberge, -n**	youth hostel
die **Kirche, -n**	church
die **Landschaft, -en**	countryside, scenery
die **Landstraße, -n**	country road
die **Luft**	air
die **Straße, -n**	road, street
die **Wiese, -n**	meadow

USEFUL PHRASES

hügelig hilly; flach flat; steil steep
ruhig peaceful
fruchtbar fertile; schlecht bad, poor
kultivieren, anbauen to cultivate, grow
fließen to flow
bummeln to wander, stroll
überqueren to cross
jagen to hunt; to shoot
in einer Jugendherberge übernachten to spend the night in a youth hostel
sich auf den Weg machen to set out, set off
der Weg zum Dorf the way to the village
in der Ferne in the distance

IMPORTANT WORDS (masculine)

der	Bach, ̈e	stream, brook
der	Bauer, -n	farmer; peasant
der	Boden, ̈	ground, earth
der	Forst, -e	forest
der	Friede(n)	peace
der	Gipfel	(mountain) top
der	Gummistiefel	wellington (boot)
der	Spazierstock, ̈e	walking stick
der	Stiefel	boot
der	Strom, ̈e	river
der	Tourist, -en	tourist
der	Wasserfall, ̈e	waterfall
der	Weg, -e	path, way, road

IMPORTANT WORDS (feminine)

die	Bäuerin	lady farmer; farmer's wife; peasant
die	Bauersfrau, -en	farmer's wife
die	Erde, -n	earth, soil
die	Gegend, -en	district, area
die	Heide, -n	heath; heather
die	Landwirtschaft	agriculture, farming
die	Talsperre, -n	dam

IMPORTANT WORDS (neuter)

das	Bauernhaus, -häuser	farmhouse
das	Fernglas, ̈er	(pair of) binoculars
das	Flachland	lowlands (pl)
das	Gebiet, -e	area
das	Gebirge	mountain chain
das	Heideland	heath
das	Heu	hay
das	Korn	corn, grain
das	Tor, -e	gate
das	Ufer	(river) bank

USEFUL WORDS (masculine)

der	Acker, ∺	field
der	Bewohner	inhabitant
der	Dorfbewohner	villager
der	Erdboden, ∺	ground
der	Jäger	hunter
der	Landwirt, -e	farmer
der	Pfad, -e	path
der	Schlamm	mud
der	Sumpf, ∺e	marsh
der	Teich, -e	pond
der	Wegweiser	signpost
der	Weiher	pond, lake
der	Weiler	hamlet
der	Weinberg, -e	vineyard
der	Wipfel	treetop

USEFUL WORDS (feminine)

die	Ebene, -n	plain
die	Ernte, -n	harvest, crop
die	Falle, -n	trap
die	Gemeinde, -n	community
die	Hecke, -n	hedge
die	Jagd, -en	hunt; hunting
die	Quelle, -n	spring; source
die	Spitze, -n	tip, peak, point
die	(Wind)mühle, -n	(wind)mill

USEFUL WORDS (neuter)

das	Geräusch, -e	noise, sound
das	Getreide	grain, cereal crop
das	Grundstück, -e	estate; plot of land
das	Heidekraut	heather
das	Loch, ∺er	hole

ESSENTIAL WORDS (masculine)

der	Ausländer	foreigner
der	Bart, ¨e	beard
der	Herr, -en	gentleman
der	Junge, -n	boy
der	Mann, ¨er	man
der	Mensch, -en	human being; man; person
der	Schnurrbart, ¨e	moustache

ESSENTIAL WORDS (feminine)

die	Ähnlichkeit, -en (mit)	similarity (to)
die	Auge, -n	eye
die	Ausländerin	foreigner
die	Bewegung, -en	movement, motion
die	Brille, -n	(pair of) glasses
die	Dame, -n	lady
die	Frau, -en	woman
die	Gesichtsfarbe, -n	complexion
die	Größe, -n	height; size
die	Hautfarbe, -n	skin colour
die	Person, -en	person
die	Schönheit	beauty

ESSENTIAL WORDS (neuter)

das	Alter	age
das	Aussehen	appearance
das	Haar, -e	hair
das	Mädchen	girl

USEFUL PHRASES

ich heiße Wolfgang my name is Wolfgang
wie heißen Sie? what is your name?
jung young; alt old
wie alt sind Sie? how old are you?, what age are you?
ich bin 16 (Jahre alt) I am 16 (years old)
mittleren Alters middle-aged

USEFUL PHRASES

bärtig **bearded**; schnurrbärtig **with a moustache**

glatt rasiert **clean-shaven**

er sieht wie sein Vater aus/wie seine Mutter aus **he looks like his father/his mother**

er ist seinem Vater/seiner Mutter ähnlich **he resembles his father/his mother**

erkennen **to recognize**

gut/schlecht aussehen **to look well/poorly**

müde/zornig/komisch aussehen **to look tired/angry/funny**

ein gut aussehender Mann **a handsome** *or* **good-looking man**

eine schöne Frau **a beautiful woman**

groß **tall, big**; klein **short, small**; lang **long**; kurz **short**

ein Mann von mittlerer Größe **a man of medium height**

sie ist 1 Meter 70 groß **she is 1 metre 70 tall**

weiß **white**; schwarz **black**; gemischtrassig **of mixed ethnic origins**

grüne/blaue/braune Augen haben **to have green/blue/brown eyes**

Kontaktlinsen/eine Brille tragen **to wear contact lenses/glasses**

er hat blonde/dunkle/schwarze/rote/graue Haare **he has blond** *or* **fair/dark/black/red/grey hair**

rothaarig **red-haired**

eine Glatze bekommen **to be going bald**

lockiges/welliges/glattes Haar **curly/wavy/straight hair**

sich benehmen **to behave (oneself)**

weinen **to cry**; lachen **to laugh**; lächeln **to smile**

vor Freude lachen/weinen **to laugh/cry with joy**

eine gute Figur haben **to have a nice figure**

wie viel wiegst du? **what do you weigh?**

die Gewohnheit haben, etw zu tun **to have a habit of doing sth**

(nicht) in der Laune *or* in der Stimmung für etw *(acc)* sein **(not) to be in the mood for sth**

gut/schlecht gelaunt **in a good/bad mood**

auf jdn böse sein **to be angry with sb**

ärgern **to annoy**

IMPORTANT WORDS (*masculine*)

der	Charakter	character
der	Gang, ¨e	walk, gait
der	Mangel, ¨	defect, fault
der	Zorn	anger

IMPORTANT WORDS (*feminine*)

die	Figur, -en	figure
die	Freude, -n	joy, delight
die	Geste, -n	gesture
die	Kontaktlinsen (*pl*)	contact lenses
die	Natur, -en	nature
die	Rasse, -n	race
die	Schüchternheit	shyness

IMPORTANT WORDS (*neuter*)

das	Gewicht, -e	weight
das	Wesen	character, personality

USEFUL WORDS (*masculine*)

der	Afrikaner	African (man)
der	Asiat, -en	Asian (man)
der	Ausdruck, ¨e	expression
der	Faulenzer	lazybones
der	Gesichtszug, ¨e	(facial) feature
der	Körperbau	build
der	Leberfleck, -e	mole
der	Muslim, -e	Muslim (man)
der	Pickel	spot, pimple
der	Pony, -s	fringe
der	Riese, -n	giant
der	Schönheitsfleck, -e	beauty spot
der	Schweiß	sweat, perspiration
der	Teint, -s	complexion
der	Turban, -e	turban
der	Zug, ¨e	feature

USEFUL WORDS *(feminine)*

die	**Afrikanerin**	African (woman)
die	**Ängstlichkeit**	nervousness
die	**Asiatin**	Asian (woman)
die	**Dauerwelle, -n**	perm
die	**Eigenschaft, -en**	quality, attribute
die	**Falte, -n**	wrinkle
die	**Faulenzerin**	lazybones
die	**Frisur, -en**	hairstyle
die	**Gestalt, -en**	figure
die	**Gewohnheit, -en**	habit
die	**Glatze, -n**	bald head
die	**Hässlichkeit**	ugliness
die	**Laune, -n**	mood, humour, temper
die	**Locke, -n**	curl
die	**Muslimin**	Muslim (woman)
die	**Narbe, -n**	scar
die	**Runzel, -n**	wrinkle
die	**Sommersprosse, -n**	freckle
die	**Stimmung, -en**	mood, frame of mind
die	**Träne, -n**	tear
die	**Wut**	fury, rage

USEFUL WORDS *(neuter)*

das	**Benehmen**	behaviour
das	**Doppelkinn, -e**	double chin
das	**Gebiss, -e**	false teeth
das	**Gefühl, -e**	feeling
das	**Gewissen**	conscience
das	**Grübchen**	dimple
das	**Kopftuch, ̈-er**	headscarf
das	**(Lebe)wesen**	creature
das	**Selbstvertrauen**	self-confidence

ähnlich (+ *dat*)	similar (to), like
ängstlich	nervous, worried
auffallend	striking
blass	pale
blind	blind
böse	angry; evil
bucklig	hunch-backed
dick	fat
dumm	stupid
dunkel	dark
dünn	thin
Durchschnitts-	average
ehrlich	honest
einsam	lonely
enttäuscht	disappointed
ernst	serious
frech (zu + *dat*)	cheeky (to)
freundlich (zu + *dat*)	friendly (to), kind (to)
froh, fröhlich	glad, happy
gebräunt	tanned
geduldig	patient
geschickt	skilful, clever
glücklich	happy
grausam	cruel
groß	tall; big
gutmütig	good-natured
hässlich	ugly
hell	fair (*skin*); light
homosexuell	homosexual
hübsch	pretty
intelligent	intelligent
klein	small
klug	clever
komisch	funny
kräftig	strong
kurz	short
kurzsichtig/weitsichtig	short-sighted/long-sighted
lächerlich	ridiculous
lahm	lame

lang	long
lesbisch	lesbian
mager	skinny, thin, lean
mürrisch	sullen
nachlässig	careless
nackt	bare, naked
nervös	nervous
nett	neat; nice
neugierig	curious, nosy
pickelig	spotty
reizend	charming
rund	round
schlank	slender
schön	beautiful
schüchtern	shy
schwach	weak
schwarz	black
seltsam	strange
sorgfältig	careful, painstaking
stark	strong
stolz (auf + acc)	proud (of)
streng	hard, harsh; strict
sympathisch	nice, likeable
tapfer	brave
taub	deaf
traurig	sad
unartig	naughty
ungeschickt	clumsy, awkward
vernünftig	sensible
verrückt	crazy, mad
verschieden	different
vorsichtig	careful, cautious
weise	wise
weiß	white
winzig	tiny
zornig	angry
zufrieden (mit + dat)	pleased (with)

ESSENTIAL WORDS *(masculine)*

der Bleistift, -e	pencil
der Computer	computer
der Direktor, -en	principal, headmaster
die Ferien *(pl)*	holidays
der Fernseher	television
der Filzstift, -e	felt-tip pen
der Freund, -e	friend
der Informatikunterricht	computer studies
der Kindergarten, ̈	nursery school
der Klassenlehrer	form teacher
der Kugelschreiber	ballpoint pen
der Kuli, -s	Biro®, ballpoint pen
der Lehrer	(school)teacher
der Preis, -e	prize
der Prüfer	examiner
der Rechner	calculator; computer
der Schreibtisch, -e	desk
der Schulanfang	beginning of term
der Schüler	schoolboy, pupil, student
der Schulfreund, -e	schoolfriend
der Schulhof, ̈e	playground
der Schulkamerad, -en	schoolfriend
der Speisesaal, -säle	dining hall
der Spielplatz, ̈e	playground
der Stundenplan, ̈e	timetable
der Taschenrechner	pocket calculator
der Test, -s	test
der Unterricht, -e	instruction; *(pl)* lessons
der Versuch, -e	experiment

ESSENTIAL WORDS *(feminine)*

die **Abschlussprüfung**	final exam
die **Antwort, -en**	answer
die **Arbeit, -en**	work; test
die **Aufgabe, -n**	exercise, task
die **Bibliothek, -en**	library
die **Biologie**	biology
die **Chemie**	chemistry
die **Direktorin**	headmistress *(of secondary school)*
die **Erdkunde**	geography
die **Frage, -n**	question
die **Freundin**	friend
die **Gemeinschaftskunde**	social studies
die **Geografie**	geography
die **Gesamtschule, -n**	comprehensive school
die **Geschichte, -n**	history; story
die **Grundschule, -n**	primary school
die **Gruppe, -n**	group
die **Handarbeit**	handicrafts; needlework
die **Hauptschule, -n**	secondary school
die **Hausaufgabe, -n**	homework
die **Karte, -n**	map; card
die **Klasse, -n**	class, form
die **Klassenarbeit, -en**	test
die **Klassenfahrt, -en**	(class) trip, outing
die **Klassenlehrerin**	form teacher
die **Kreide**	chalk
die **Kunst**	art
die **Lehrerin**	(school)teacher
die **Mappe, -n**	briefcase; folder
die **Mathematik; die Mathe**	mathematics, maths
die **Mittagspause, -n**	lunch break
die **Musik**	music
die **Pause, -n**	break, interval
die **Physik**	physics

USEFUL PHRASES

die Schule besuchen to attend school
in der Schule at school
ich gehe in die Schule I'm going to school
arbeiten to work
aufpassen to pay attention; zuhören to listen
lernen to learn; studieren to study; vergessen to forget
lesen to read; schreiben to write; sprechen to speak
sprichst du Deutsch? do you speak German?
seit wie vielen Jahren lernen Sie Deutsch? how many years have you been
    learning German?
ich lerne seit 3 Jahren Deutsch I've been learning German for 3 years
lehren, unterrichten to teach
ich möchte Lehrer werden I'd like to be a teacher
der Französischlehrer the French teacher (*teacher of French*)
eine Prüfung machen to sit an exam
das Abitur machen to sit one's A-levels (*approx*)
wiederholen to repeat; to revise
mündlich oral; schriftlich written
eine Prüfung bestehen/nicht bestehen to pass/fail an exam
den ersten Preis gewinnen to win first prize
durchfallen to fail
sitzen bleiben to repeat a year
Fortschritte machen to make progress
versetzen to move *or* put up
die Schule verlassen to leave school
klug clever; intelligent intelligent; dumm stupid
fragen to ask; antworten to answer, reply
jdm eine Frage stellen to ask sb a question
eine Frage beantworten to answer a question

ESSENTIAL WORDS (*feminine continued*)

die	**Prüfung, -en**	exam, examination
die	**Realschule, -n**	secondary school
die	**(höhere) Schule, (-n) -n**	(secondary) school
die	**Schülerin**	schoolgirl, pupil; student
die	**Schulfreundin** *or*	schoolfriend
	die **Schulkameradin**	
die	**Schultasche, -n**	satchel, school bag
die	**Schuluniform, -en**	school uniform
die	**Seite, -n**	page
die	**Sozialkunde**	social studies
die	**Tafel, -n**	blackboard
die	**Technik**	technology
die	**Tinte**	ink
die	**Turnhalle, -n**	gym, gymnasium
die	**Universität, -en; die Uni**	university

ESSENTIAL WORDS (*neuter*)

das	**Buch, ⸚er**	book
das	**Deutsch**	German
das	**Englisch**	English
das	**Examen, -** *or* **Examina**	exam, examination
das	**Französisch**	French
das	**Gymnasium, -ien**	grammar school
das	**Klassenzimmer**	classroom, schoolroom
das	**Lineal, -e**	ruler
das	**Papier, -e**	paper
das	**(Schul)fach, ⸚er**	(school) subject
das	**(Schul)heft, -e**	exercise book
das	**Semester**	term (2 *per year*)
das	**Technisches Zeichnen Spanisch**	technical drawing Spanish
das	**Trimester**	term (3 *per year*)
das	**Turnen**	P.E.; gymnastics
das	**Werken**	handicrafts
das	**Wörterbuch, ⸚er**	dictionary

IMPORTANT WORDS (masculine)

der	**Austausch, -e**	exchange
der	**Buchstabe, -n**	letter of alphabet
der	**Erfolg, -e**	success
der	**Ethikunterricht**	ethics
der	**Fehler**	mistake, error; fault
der	**Hochschüler**	college student
der	**Klassenkamerad, -en**	classmate
der	**Klassensprecher**	form prefect
der	**Kurs, -e**	course
der	**Mitschüler**	classmate, schoolmate
der	**Radiergummi, -s**	rubber, eraser
der	**Rektor, -en**	headmaster *(primary)*; rector
der	**Schlafsaal, -säle**	dormitory
der	**Schülerlotse, -n**	*pupil who helps with school crossing patrol*
der	**Student, -en**	student
der	**Zettel**	piece of paper; note; form

IMPORTANT WORDS (neuter)

das	**Abitur**	German school-leaving certificate/exam
das	**Bestehen**	pass *(in exam)*
das	**Blatt, ¨er**	sheet *(of paper)*
das	**Diplom, -e**	diploma
das	**Ergebnis, -se**	result *(of exam)*
das	**Italienisch**	Italian
das	**Klassenbuch, ¨er**	class register
das	**Latein**	Latin
das	**Lehrerzimmer**	staff room
das	**Pflichtfach, ¨er**	compulsory subject
das	**Rechnen**	arithmetic
das	**(Schul)zeugnis, -se**	(school) report
das	**(Sprach)labor, -e**	(language) lab
das	**Vokabular**	vocabulary
das	**Wahlfach, ¨er**	option, optional subject
das	**Zeichnen**	drawing *(subject)*

IMPORTANT WORDS *(feminine)*

die	Algebra	algebra
die	Aula, Aulen *or* -s	assembly hall
die	Berufsschule, -n	vocational *or* trade school
die	Fach(hoch)schule, -n	technical college
die	Fremdsprache, -n	foreign language
die	Ganztagsschule, -n	all-day school *or* schooling
die	Garderobe, -n	cloakroom
die	gemischte Schule, -n -n	mixed school, co-ed
die	Geometrie	geometry
die	Grammatik	grammar
die	Halbtagsschule, -n	half-day school
die	Hochschule, -n	college; university
die	Klassenkameradin	classmate
die	Lehre	teaching
die	Leistung, -en	achievement
die	Methode, -n	method
die	Mitschülerin	classmate, schoolmate
die	mittlere Reife	intermediate school-leaving certificate/exam
die	Nachhilfe	private coaching *or* tuition
die	Naturwissenschaft, -en	natural history
die	Note, -n	mark, grade
die	Oberstufe, -n	upper school
die	Reihe, -n	row (*of seats etc*)
die	Rektorin	headmistress (*primary*)
die	Religion	religion
die	Schülermitverwaltung, -en (SMV)	school *or* student council
die	Sprache, -n	language
die	neueren Sprachen (*pl*)	modern languages
die	Strafarbeit, -en	punishment exercise
die	Studentin	student
die	Technische Hochschule, -n -n	technical college
die	Übersetzung, -en	translation
die	Übung, -en	practice; exercise
die	Zeichnung, -en	drawing (*piece of work*)

USEFUL WORDS (*masculine*)

die	Abwesenden (*pl*)	absentees
die	Anwesenden (*pl*)	those present
der	Aufsatz, ⁻e	composition, essay
der	Aufsichtsschüler	prefect
der	Bericht, -e	report
der	Bleistiftspitzer	pencil sharpener
der	Drehbleistift, -e	propelling pencil
der	Federhalter	(fountain) pen
die	Fortschritte (*pl*)	progress
der	Füllfederhalter; der Füller	fountain pen
der	Gang, ⁻e	corridor
der	Gesang	singing
der	Internatsschüler	boarder
der	Irrtum, ⁻er	error
der	Klecks, -e	blot, stain
der	Religionsunterricht	religious education
der	Satz, ⁻e	sentence
der	Tageslichtprojektor, -en	overhead projector
der	Tagesschüler	day-boy
der	Vortrag, ⁻e	talk, lecture

USEFUL PHRASES

schwierig difficult; einfach easy
interessant interesting; langweilig boring
faul lazy; fleißig hard-working; streng strict
mein Lieblingsfach my favourite subject
letztes Jahr habe ich einen Austausch gemacht I did an exchange last year
schulfrei haben to have a day off
hitzefrei haben to have a day off because of very hot weather

USEFUL WORDS *(feminine)*

die	Aktentasche, -n	briefcase
die	Aufsichtsschülerin	prefect
die	Dichtung	poetry
die	Doppelstunde, -n	double period
die	Erziehung	education, schooling
die	Handelsschule, -n	commercial college
die	Hauswirtschaft	home economics
die	Internatsschülerin	boarder
die	Kantine, -n	canteen
die	Lektion, -en	lesson, unit
die	Lektüre, -n	reading
die	Pädagogische Hochschule, -n -n (PH)	College of Education
die	Preisverleihung, -en	prize-giving
die	Rechtschreibung	spelling
die	Regel, -n	rule
die	Tagesschülerin	day-girl
die	Vorlesung, -en	lecture

USEFUL WORDS *(neuter)*

das	Benehmen	behaviour, conduct
das	Diktat, -e	dictation
das	Griechisch	Greek
das	Internat, -e	boarding school
das	Nachsitzen	detention
das	Notizbuch, ¨er	jotter; notebook
das	Pult, -e	desk
das	Russisch	Russian
das	Studenten(wohn)heim, -e	students' hall of residence
das	Tonbandgerät, -e	tape recorder

USEFUL PHRASES

abschreiben to copy
die Schule schwänzen to skip school
bestrafen to punish; loben to praise
jdn nachsitzen lassen to keep sb in (after school)

ESSENTIAL WORDS (masculine)

der	Abfall, ˝e	waste
der	Baum, Bäume	tree
der	Berg, -e	hill, mountain
der	Energieverbrauch	energy consumption
der	Fisch, -e	fish
der	Fluss, ˝e	river
der	Müll	rubbish, refuse
der	Regen	rain
der	saure Regen	acid rain
der	Schadstoff, -e	harmful substance
der	See, -n	lake
der	Smog	smog
der	Umweltschutz	conservation
der	Strand, ˝e	beach
der	Wald, ˝er	forest, wood

ESSENTIAL WORDS (feminine)

die	Atmosphäre	atmosphere
die	Blume, -n	flower
die	Fabrik, -en	factory
die	Flasche, -n	bottle
die	Frage, -n	question
die	globale Erwärmung	global warming
die	Insel, -n	island
die	Krise, -n	crisis
die	Luft	air
die	Ozonschicht	ozone layer
die	See, -n	sea
die	Temperatur, -en	temperature
die	Welt	world
die	Windenergie	wind energy
die	Windfarm, -en	wind farm
die	Zeit, -en	time
die	Zeitschrift, -en	magazine
die	Zeitung, -en	newspaper

ESSENTIAL WORDS *(neuter)*

das	**Auto, -s**	car
das	**Benzin**	petrol
das	**Essen**	food
das	**Gas, -e**	gas
das	**Gemüse**	vegetables
das	**Glas**	glass
das	**Land, ̈er**	country
das	**Meer, -e**	ocean; sea
das	**Obst**	fruit
das	**Ozonloch, ̈er**	hole in the ozone layer
das	**Schwermetall, -e**	heavy metal
das	**Tier, -e**	animal
das	**Treibgas, -e**	propellant
das	**Waldsterben**	dying of the forests
das	**Wasser**	water
das	**Wetter**	weather

USEFUL PHRASES

eine Weltreise machen **to go round the world**
das höchste/größte/schönste ... der Welt **the highest/biggest/
   most beautiful ... in the world**
in der Zukunft **in future**
aussterben **to become extinct**
verschmutzen **to pollute**
zerstören **to destroy**
verunreinigen **to contaminate**
etw verbieten **to ban sth**
retten **to save**
wieder aufbereiten **to reprocess**
wieder verwerten, recyceln **to recycle**
biologisch abbaubar **biodegradable**
umweltfreundlich **environment-friendly**
umweltschädlich **harmful to the environment**
grün **green**; ökologisch **ecological**
organisch **organic**; bleifrei **unleaded**

IMPORTANT WORDS (masculine)

die	Grünen (pl)	the Greens
der	Kanal, Kanäle	canal
der	Mond	moon
der	Müllabladeplatz, ̈-e	rubbish tip or dump
der	Planet, -en	planet
die	tropischen Regenwälder (pl)	tropical rainforests
der	Strom, ̈-e	river

IMPORTANT WORDS (feminine)

die	Chemikalien (pl)	chemicals
die	Erde	the earth
die	Gegend, -en	region, area
die	Hitze	heat
die	Katastrophe, -n	catastrophe
die	Kernkraft	nuclear power
die	Küste, -n	coast
die	Lösung, -en	solution
die	Pflanze, -n	plant
die	Solaranlage, -n	solar power plant
die	Sprühdose, -n	aerosol
die	Wiederverwertung	recycling, reprocessing
die	Zukunft	future

IMPORTANT WORDS (neuter)

das	Aluminium	aluminium
das	Deodorant -s or -e	deodorant
das	Gebiet, -e	area
das	Kernkraftwerk, -e	nuclear power station
das	Klima, -s or -te	climate
das	Ökosystem	ecosystem
das	Produkt, -e	product; (pl) produce
das	Recycling	recycling
das	Spülmittel	washing-up liquid
das	Waschmittel	detergent
das	Waschpulver	washing powder

USEFUL WORDS (masculine)

die **Bodenschätze** (pl)	mineral resources
der **Bohrturm, ̈e**	drilling or oil rig
der **Brennstoff, -e**	fuel (for heating)
der **Dieselkraftstoff**	diesel oil
der **Elektrosmog**	electromagnetic radiation
der **FCKW, -s**	CFC
der **Ökologe, -n**	ecologist
der **Ozean, -e**	ocean
der **Recyclinghof, ̈e**	recycling plant
der **Schaden, ̈**	damage, harm
der **Treibhauseffekt**	greenhouse effect
der **Treibstoff, -e**	fuel (for vehicles)
der **Umweltschützer**	conservationist, environmentalist

USEFUL WORDS (feminine)

die **Lärmbelästigung**	noise pollution
die **Luftverschmutzung**	air pollution
die **Mülldeponie, -n**	waste disposal site
die **Ökologin**	ecologist
die **Steuer, -n**	tax
die **Umwelt**	environment
die **(Umwelt)verschmutzung**	(environmental) pollution
die **Wiederaufarbeitungsanlage, -n**	reprocessing plant
die **Windkraft**	wind power
die **Wüste, -n**	desert

USEFUL WORDS (neuter)

das **Abgas**	exhaust fumes
die **Abwässer** (pl)	sewage
das **Altpapier**	waste paper
das **Erdbeben**	earthquake
das **Loch, ̈er**	hole
das **Weltall**	universe

ESSENTIAL WORDS *(masculine)*

	Alte(r), -n	old man/woman
der	**Babysitter**	babysitter
der	**Bruder, ⸚**	brother
die	**Eltern** *(pl)*	parents
	Erwachsene(r), -n	grown-up, adult
der	**Familienname, -n**	surname
der	**Freund, -e**	friend
die	**Geschwister** *(pl)*	brothers and sisters
die	**Großeltern** *(pl)*	grandparents
der	**Großvater, ⸚**	grandfather
der	**Junge, -n**	boy
die	**Leute** *(pl)*	people
der	**Mädchenname, -n**	maiden name
der	**Mann, ⸚er**	man; husband
der	**junge Mann, -n ⸚er**	youth, young man
der	**Mensch, -en**	human being, person
der	**Name, -n**	name
der	**Onkel**	uncle
der	**Opa, -s; der Opi, -s**	grandpa
der	**Sohn, ⸚e**	son
der	**Vater, ⸚**	father
der	**Vati, -s**	dad, daddy
der	**Vorname, -n**	first name, Christian name
der	**Zwilling, -e**	twin
der	**Zwillingsbruder, ⸚**	twin brother

USEFUL PHRASES

ich heiße Karl **my name is Karl**
ich bin 17 (Jahre alt) **I am 17 (years old)**
ich bin 1986 geboren **I was born in 1986**
wie heißt du? – wie alt bist du? **what's your name? – how old are you?**
männlich **male**; weiblich **female**
kennen **to know**; kennen lernen **to get to know**
vorstellen **to introduce**; erinnern (an + *acc*) **to remind (of)**
unsere Familie stammt aus Polen **our family comes from Poland**
wir wohnen jetzt in Österreich **we live in Austria now**

ESSENTIAL WORDS *(feminine)*

die Dame, -n	lady
die Familie, -n	family
die Frau, -en	woman; wife
die Freundin	friend
die Großmutter, ˙˙	grandmother
die Hausfrau, -en	housewife
die Mutter, ˙˙	mother
die Mutti, -s	mum, mummy
die Oma, -s; die Omi, -s	granny
die Person, -en	person
die Schwester, -n	sister
die Tante, -n	aunt
die Tochter, ˙˙	daughter
die Zwillingsschwester, -n	twin sister

ESSENTIAL WORDS *(neuter)*

das Alter	age; old age
das Baby, -s	baby
das Einzelkind, -er	only child
das Fräulein	young lady
das Kind, -er	child
das Mädchen	(young) girl
das Paar, -e	couple

USEFUL PHRASES

verlobt engaged; verheiratet married
ledig single; geschieden divorced
meine Eltern leben getrennt my parents are separated
sich verloben to get engaged; sich verheiraten to get married
sich scheiden lassen to get divorced
älter/jünger als ich older/younger than me
die ganze Familie the whole family
bei uns at our place, at our house
mein Großvater ist 1990 gestorben my grandfather died in 1990
tot dead; streiten to quarrel; sich vertragen to get along

IMPORTANT WORDS (*masculine*)

der	Austauschpartner	partner (*in an exchange*)
	Bekannte(r), -n	acquaintance
der	Cousin, -s	cousin
der	Ehemann, ⁀er	married man; husband
der	Enkel	grandson; (*pl*) grandchildren
	Jugendliche(r), -n	teenager, young person
der	Nachbar, -n	neighbour
der	Nachname, -n	surname
der	Neffe, -n	nephew
der	Rentner	(old age) pensioner
der	Schwiegersohn, ⁀e	son-in-law
der	Schwiegervater, ⁀	father-in-law
	Verlobte(r), -n	fiancé/fiancée
	Verwandte(r), -n	relation, relative
der	Vetter, -n	cousin
der	Witwer	widower

IMPORTANT WORDS (*feminine*)

die	Cousine, -n	cousin
die	Ehefrau, -en	married woman; wife
die	Enkelin	granddaughter
die	Jugend	youth (*stage of life*)
die	Kusine, -n	cousin
die	Nachbarin	neighbour
die	Nichte, -n	niece
die	Rentnerin	(old age) pensioner
die	Schwiegermutter, ⁀	mother-in-law
die	Schwiegertochter, ⁀	daughter-in-law
die	Witwe, -n	widow

IMPORTANT WORDS (*neuter*)

das	Aupairmädchen	au pair
das	Ehepaar, -e	married couple
das	Enkelkind, -er	grandchild
das	Kindermädchen	nanny

USEFUL WORDS *(masculine)*

der	**Bräutigam, -e**	bridegroom
die	**Drillinge** *(pl)*	triplets
der	**Elternteil, -e**	parent
der	**Geburtsort, -e**	place of birth
der	**Junggeselle, -n**	bachelor
die	**Jungverheirateten** *(pl)*	newly-weds
der	**Pate, -n**	godfather
der	**Rufname, -n**	first name, usual name
der	**Säugling, -e**	baby, infant
der	**Schwager, ∵**	brother-in-law
der	**Spitzname, -n**	nickname
der	**Stiefbruder, ∵**	stepbrother
der	**Stiefvater, ∵**	stepfather
der	**Vorfahr, -en**	ancestor
der	**Vormund, -e** or **∵er**	guardian
der	**Zuname, -n**	surname

USEFUL WORDS *(feminine)*

die	**Braut, Bräute**	bride
die	**Hochzeit, -en**	wedding
die	**alte Jungfer, -n -n**	spinster, old maid
die	**Junggesellin**	unmarried woman
die	**Patin**	godmother
die	**Schwägerin**	sister-in-law
die	**Stiefmutter, ∵**	stepmother
die	**Stiefschwester, -n**	stepsister
die	**Waise, -n**	orphan

USEFUL WORDS *(neuter)*

das	**Geburtsdatum, -daten**	date of birth
das	**Greisenalter**	(extreme) old age
das	**Waisenhaus, -häuser**	orphanage
das	**Weib, -er**	woman *(old-fashioned or pejorative)*

ESSENTIAL WORDS (*masculine*)

der	**Bauer, -n**	farmer; peasant, countryman
der	**Bauernhof, ⁻e**	farm, farmyard
der	**Hahn, ⁻e**	cock, rooster
der	**Hügel**	hill
der	**Hund, -e**	dog
der	**Landarbeiter**	farm labourer
der	**Markt, ⁻e**	market
der	**Wald, ⁻er**	wood, forest

ESSENTIAL WORDS (*feminine*)

die	**Bäuerin**	lady farmer; farmer's wife; peasant
die	**Bauersfrau, -en**	farmer's wife
die	**Ente, -n**	duck
die	**Erde**	earth, soil
die	**Gans, ⁻e**	goose
die	**Henne, -n**	hen
die	**(Heu)gabel, -n**	pitchfork
die	**Katze, -n**	cat
die	**Wiese, -n**	meadow

ESSENTIAL WORDS (*neuter*)

das	**Dorf, ⁻er**	village
das	**Feld, -er**	field
das	**Kalb, ⁻er**	calf
das	**Land, ⁻er**	land; country
das	**Tier, -e**	animal

USEFUL PHRASES

auf einem Bauernhof wohnen to live on a farm
Ferien auf dem Bauernhof farm holidays
der Bauer sorgt für die Tiere the farmer looks after the animals
die Felder pflügen to plough the fields
die Ernte einbringen to bring in the harvest or the crops
zur Erntezeit at harvest-time

IMPORTANT WORDS (masculine)

der	Bach, ̈-e	stream, brook
der	Boden, ̈-	ground, earth; floor; loft
der	Bulle, -n	bull
der	Lieferwagen	van
der	Ochse, -n	ox
der	Ökobauer, -n	organic farmer
der	Puter	turkey(-cock)
der	Traktor, -en	tractor
der	Weizen	wheat
der	Zaun, Zäune	fence

IMPORTANT WORDS (feminine)

die	Feldmaus, -mäuse	fieldmouse
die	Heide, -n	heath
die	Herde, -n	herd; flock
die	Kuh, ̈-e	cow
die	Landschaft, -en	countryside, scenery
die	Landwirtschaft	agriculture, farming
die	Milchkanne, -n	milk churn
die	Ökobäuerin	organic farmer
die	Pute, -n	turkey(-hen)

IMPORTANT WORDS (neuter)

das	Bauernhaus, -häuser	farmhouse
das	Gebäude	building
das	Heu	hay
das	Huhn, ̈-er	chicken, hen; (pl) poultry
das	Hühnerhaus, -häuser	henhouse
das	Korn, ̈-er	corn, grain
das	Lamm, ̈-er	lamb
das	Pferd, -e	horse
das	Schaf, -e	sheep
das	Schwein, -e	pig
das	Stroh	straw

USEFUL WORDS *(masculine)*

der	**Acker,** ¨	field
der	**Brunnen**	well
der	**Dünger**	dung, manure; fertilizer
der	**Eimer**	bucket, pail
der	**Esel**	donkey
der	**Graben,** ¨	ditch
der	**Hafer**	oats *(pl)*
der	**Hase, -n**	hare
der	**Haufen**	heap, pile
der	**Heuboden,** ¨	hayloft
der	**Karren**	cart
der	**Kuhstall,** ¨**e**	cowshed, byre
der	**Landwirt, -e**	farmer
der	**Mähdrescher**	combine harvester
der	**Mais**	maize
der	**Pferdestall,** ¨**e**	stable
der	**Pflug,** ¨**e**	plough
der	**Roggen**	rye
der	**Schäfer**	shepherd
der	**Schäferhund, -e**	sheepdog, German shepherd
der	**Schlamm**	mud
der	**Schuppen**	shed
der	**Stall,** ¨**e**	stable; sty; (hen)house
der	**Stapel**	pile
der	**Staub**	dust
der	**Stier, -e**	bull
der	**Teich, -e**	pond
der	**Truthahn,** ¨**e**	turkey(-cock)
der	**Widder**	ram

USEFUL WORDS *(feminine)*

die	**Ernte, -n**	harvest, crop
die	**Erntezeit, -en**	harvest (time)
die	**Furche, -n**	furrow
die	**Garbe, -n**	sheaf
die	**Gerste**	barley
die	**Kleie**	bran
die	**Leiter, -n**	ladder
die	**Scheune, -n**	barn
die	**Vogelscheuche, -n**	scarecrow
die	**Weide, -n**	pasture
die	**(Wind)mühle, -n**	(wind)mill
die	**Ziege, -n**	goat

USEFUL WORDS *(neuter)*

das	**Gatter**	gate; railing
das	**Geflügel**	poultry
das	**Geschirr, -e**	harness
das	**Getreide**	cereals, grain
das	**Küken**	chicken, chick
das	**(Rind)vieh**	cattle *(pl)*, livestock
das	**Zugpferd, -e**	carthorse

USEFUL PHRASES

genmanipulierte Lebensmittel **genetically modified food**
organisch **organic**
Eier aus Freilandhaltung **free-range eggs**
aus biologischem Anbau **organically grown**

ESSENTIAL + IMPORTANT WORDS (masculine)

der Fisch, -e	fish
der Goldfisch, -e	goldfish
der Schwanz, ¨e	tail

USEFUL WORDS (masculine)

der Aal, -e	eel
der Floh, ¨e	flea
der Flügel	wing
der Frosch, ¨e	frog
der Hai(fisch), -e	shark
der Hecht, -e	pike
der Hering, -e	herring
der Hummer	lobster
der Kabeljau, -e or -s	cod
der Käfer	beetle
der Krebs, -e	crab; crayfish
der Lachs, -e	salmon
der Maikäfer	cockchafer
der Marienkäfer	ladybird
der Nachtfalter	moth
der Schellfisch, -e	haddock
der Schmetterling, -e	butterfly
der Stich, -e	sting
der Thunfisch, -e	tuna fish
der Tintenfisch, -e	(small) octopus, squid
der Weißfisch, -e	whiting
der Wurm, ¨er	worm

ESSENTIAL + IMPORTANT WORDS (neuter)

das Insekt, -en	insect
das Schalentier, -e	shellfish
das Wasser	water

USEFUL PHRASES

im Wasser schwimmen to swim in the water
in der Luft fliegen to fly in the air
„Angeln verboten" "no fishing"

ESSENTIAL + IMPORTANT WORDS *(feminine)*

die **Biene, -n**	bee
die **Fliege, -n**	fly
die **Forelle, -n**	trout
die **Luft**	air
die **Sardine, -n**	sardine
die **Wespe, -n**	wasp

USEFUL WORDS *(feminine)*

die **Ameise, -n**	ant
die **Auster, -n**	oyster
die **Flosse, -n**	fin
die **Garnele, -n**	shrimp; prawn
die **Grille, -n**	cricket
die **Heuschrecke, -n**	grasshopper
die **Hornisse, -n**	hornet
die **Kaulquappe, -n**	tadpole
die **Kiemen** *(pl)*	gills
die **Krabbe, -n**	shrimp; prawn
die **Languste, -n**	crayfish
die **Libelle, -n**	dragonfly
die **(Mies)muschel, -n**	mussel
die **Motte, -n**	moth
die **Mücke, -n**	midge
die **Qualle, -n**	jellyfish
die **Raupe, -n**	caterpillar
die **Schmeißfliege, -n**	bluebottle
die **Schuppe, -n**	scale
die **Seezunge, -n**	sole
die **Seidenraupe, -n**	silkworm
die **Spinne, -n**	spider
die **Stechmücke, -n**	mosquito
die **Wanze, -n**	bug

USEFUL PHRASES

stechen **to sting**
die Biene/die Wespe sticht **the bee/the wasp stings**
die Mücke sticht **the midge bites**

ESSENTIAL WORDS *(masculine)*

der	Alkohol	alcohol
der	(Apfel)saft, ̈-e	(apple) juice
der	Apfelstrudel	apple strudel
der	Apfelwein, -e	cider
der	Appetit, -e	appetite
der	Aufschnitt, -e	cold meats
der	Becher	mug; tumbler
die	Chips *(pl)*	crisps
der	Durst	thirst
der	Eintopf, ̈-e	stew
der	Essig	vinegar
der	Fisch, -e	fish
der	Honig	honey
der	Hunger	hunger
der	Imbiss, -e	snack
der	Joghurt, -s	yoghurt
der	Kaffee	coffee
der	Kakao, -s	cocoa
der	Käse	cheese
der	Keks, -e	biscuit
der	Kellner	waiter
der	Kuchen	cake
der	Löffel	spoon
der	Nachtisch, -e	dessert, sweet
der	Orangensaft	orange juice
der	Pfeffer	pepper
der	Reis	rice
der	Salat, -e	salad
der	Schinken	ham
der	Schnellimbiss, -e	snack bar
der	Senf, -e	mustard
der	Sprudel	sparkling mineral water
der	Tee, -s	tea
der	Teller	plate
der	Tisch, -e	table
der	Wein, -e	wine
der	Zucker	sugar

USEFUL PHRASES

essen to eat; trinken to drink
könnte ich bitte eine Cola haben? could I have a Coke please?
wie wär's mit einem Apfelsaft? do you fancy an apple juice?
bezahlen bitte! the bill please!
schlucken to swallow; schmecken to taste (good)
probieren to try
das schmeckt ihm he likes it
schmeckt Ihnen der Wein? do you like the wine?
das schmeckt scheußlich! that tastes dreadful!
ich esse gern Käse I like (eating) cheese
ich trinke gern Tee I like (drinking) tea
ich mag Käse/Tee nicht, ich mag keinen Käse/Tee I don't like cheese/tea
ich esse lieber Brot/trinke lieber Bier I prefer bread/beer
hungrig sein, Hunger haben to be hungry
durstig sein, Durst haben to be thirsty
ich sterbe vor Hunger! I'm starving!
hast du schon gegessen? have you eaten yet?
frühstücken to have breakfast
vorbereiten to prepare; kochen to cook; backen to bake; braten to fry;
    grillen to grill; würzen to season
paniert in breadcrumbs
schneiden to cut; streichen to spread
einschenken to pour (tea etc)
bitten um to ask for; reichen to pass, hand on
Mahlzeit!, guten Appetit! enjoy your meal!
bedienen Sie sich!, nehmen Sie sich! help yourselves!
alkoholisch alcoholic; alkoholfrei non-alcoholic
den Tisch decken/abräumen to lay or set/clear the table
abwaschen, (das Geschirr) spülen to wash up, do the dishes
abtrocknen to dry the dishes

ESSENTIAL WORDS *(feminine)*

die	**Bedienung**	service; service charge
die	**Bestellung, -en**	order
die	**Bockwurst, -würste**	*type of pork sausage*
die	**(Braten)soße, -n**	gravy
die	**Bratwurst, -würste**	grilled *or* fried sausage
die	**Butter**	butter
die	**Cola**	Coke®
die	**Currywurst, -würste**	curried sausage
die	**Dose, -n**	box; tin, can
die	**Erfrischung, -en**	refreshment
die	**Flasche, -n**	bottle
die	**Frucht, ̈e**	(piece of) fruit
die	**Gabel, -n**	fork
die	**Imbissstube, -n**	snack bar
die	**Kaffeekanne, -n**	coffee pot
die	**Kartoffel, -n**	potato
die	**Kellnerin**	waitress
die	**Leberwurst**	liver sausage
die	**Limonade, -n**, die **Limo**	lemonade
die	**Mahlzeit, -en**	meal
die	**Margarine, -n**	margarine
die	**Milch**	milk
die	**Nachspeise, -n**	dessert, sweet
die	**Pizza, -s**	pizza
die	**kalte Platte, -n -n**	cold meal
die	**Portion, -en**	portion, helping
die	**Praline, -n**	*(individual)* chocolate
die	**Rechnung, -en**	bill
die	**Sahne**	cream
die	**Salzkartoffeln** *(pl)*	boiled potatoes
die	**Schlagsahne**	whipped cream
die	**Schokolade, -n**	chocolate
die	**Soße, -n**	sauce
die	**Speisekarte, -n**	menu
die	**Suppe, -n**	soup
die	**Tageskarte, -n**	today's menu
die	**Tasse, -n**	cup

ESSENTIAL WORDS *(neuter)*

das	Abendbrot	supper
das	Abendessen	evening meal
das	Bier, -e	beer
das	Bonbon, -s	sweet, sweetie
das	(Brat)hähnchen	(roast) chicken
das	Brot, -e	bread; loaf
ein	belegtes Brot, -n -e	open sandwich
das	Brötchen	(bread) roll
das	Butterbrot, -e	piece of bread and butter
das	Café, -s	café
das	Ei, -er	egg
das	Eis	ice cream
das	Essen	meal
das	Feuerzeug, -e	lighter
das	Fleisch	meat
das	Frühstück, -e	breakfast
das	Gemüse	vegetables
das	Getränk, -e	drink
das	Glas, ̈-er	glass
das	Graubrot, -e	brown bread
das	Gulasch	goulash
das	Kalbfleisch	veal
das	Kotelett, -e	chop
das	Menü, -s	menu
das	Messer	knife
das	Mineralwasser	mineral water
das	Mittagessen	lunch; dinner
das	Obst	fruit
das	Öl	oil
das	Omelett, -s	omelette
das	Picknick, -s *or* -e	picnic
das	Pils	lager
die	Pommes frites *(pl)*	chips, French fries
das	Restaurant, -s	restaurant
das	Rindfleisch	beef
das	Rührei	scrambled egg

ESSENTIAL WORDS *(feminine continued)*

die **Teekanne, -n**	teapot
die **Torte, -n**	flan, tart, cake
die **Untertasse, -n**	saucer
die **Wurst, ̈e**	sausage
die **Zigarette, -n**	cigarette
die **Zigarre, -n**	cigar

ESSENTIAL WORDS *(neuter continued)*

das **Salz**	salt
das **Schnitzel**	(veal) cutlet
das **Schwarzbrot**	rye bread
das **Schweinefleisch**	pork
das **Spiegelei, -er**	fried egg
das **Steak, -s**	steak
das **Wasser**	water
das **Weißbrot, -e**	white bread
das **Wiener Schnitzel**	Wiener schnitzel
das **Wirtshaus, -häuser**	inn
das **Würstchen**	frankfurter

USEFUL PHRASES
das schmeckt sehr gut **this tastes very nice**
prost! **cheers!**
mit jdm anstoßen **to clink glasses with sb**
süß **sweet**; salzig **salty**; sauer **sour**

IMPORTANT WORDS (masculine)

der	Aschenbecher	ashtray
der	Champagner	champagne
der	Dessertlöffel	dessert spoon
der	Döner	kebab
der	Einkaufswagen	shopping trolley
der	Esslöffel	tablespoon
der	Geschmack, ¨e	taste
der	Hamburger	hamburger
der	Kaugummi, -s	chewing gum
der	Knoblauch	garlic
der	Knödel	dumpling
der	Kognak, -s	brandy
der	Korken	cork
der	Rindsbraten	roast beef
der	Schnaps, ¨e	schnapps; spirits
der	Sekt, -e	champagne
der	Stammtisch, -e	*table for the regulars*
der	Strohhalm, -e	(drinking) straw
der	Tabak	tobacco
der	Teelöffel	teaspoon
der	Toast, -s	toast
der	Whisky, -s	whisky

USEFUL PHRASES

rauchen to smoke
danke, ich rauche nicht no thanks, I don't smoke
„Rauchen verboten" "no smoking"
um Feuer bitten to ask for a light
anzünden to light up
ich versuche, das Rauchen aufzugeben I'm trying to give up smoking

IMPORTANT WORDS (feminine)

die	Auswahl (an + dat)	choice (of)
die	Gaststätte, -n	restaurant; pub
die	Getränkekarte, -n	wine list
die	Kneipe, -n	pub
die	Krabben (pl)	shrimps; prawns
die	Marmelade, -n	jam
die	Majonäse, -n	mayonnaise
die	Meeresfrüchte (pl)	seafood, shellfish
die	Nudeln (pl)	pasta, noodles
die	Orangenmarmelade, -n	marmalade
die	Salami, -s	salami
die	Salatsoße, -n	salad dressing
die	Schale, -n	bowl
die	Scheibe, -n	slice
die	Schüssel, -n	bowl, dish
die	Theke, -n	bar; counter
die	Vanillesoße, -n	custard
die	Vorspeise, -n	hors d'œuvre, starter
die	Weinkarte, -n	wine list
die	Wirtschaft, -en	pub

IMPORTANT WORDS (neuter)

das	Geflügel	poultry
das	Gericht, -e	dish, course
das	Geschirr	dishes, crockery
das	Hauptgericht, -e	main course
das	Lammfleisch	lamb
das	Mus	purée
das	Rezept, -e	recipe
das	Sandwich, -es	sandwich
das	Tablett, -e	tray
das	Trinkgeld, -er	tip

USEFUL PHRASES

bestellen to order

was können Sie mir empfehlen? what do you recommend?

USEFUL WORDS (masculine)

der	**Eiswürfel**	ice cube
der	**Kaffeefilter**	coffee-maker
der	**Kamillentee**	camomile tea
der	**Kartoffelbrei**	mashed potatoes (pl)
der	**Kartoffelsalat**	potato salad
der	**Krug (¨e) Wasser**	jug of water
der	**Pfannkuchen**	pancake
der	**Pudding**	blancmange
der	**Rahm**	cream
der	**Rotwein**	red wine
der	**(Schinken)speck**	bacon
der	**Teebeutel**	tea bag
der	**Wackelpeter**	jelly
der	**Weinbrand, ¨e**	brandy
der	**Weißwein**	white wine
der	**Zwieback**	toast (in packets)

USEFUL WORDS (feminine)

die	**Büchse, -n**	tin, can
die	**Eisdiele, -n**	ice cream parlour
die	**Frikadelle, -n**	rissole
die	**Konserven (pl)**	preserved foods
die	**Niere, -n**	kidney
die	**Pfeife, -n**	pipe
die	**Serviette, -n**	napkin, serviette
die	**Thermosflasche, -n**	flask

USEFUL WORDS (neuter)

das	**Besteck**	cutlery
das	**Geflügel**	poultry
das	**Kartoffelpüree**	mashed potatoes
das	**Mehl, -e**	flour
das	**Streichholz, ¨er**	match
das	**Tischtuch, ¨er**	tablecloth
das	**Wild**	game (meat)

ESSENTIAL WORDS *(masculine)*

der	Ausflug, ⸚e	outing, trip
der	Besuch, -e	visit; visitor
der	Brieffreund, -e	penfriend
der	Computer	computer
der	Fan, -s	fan
der	Film, -e	film
der	(Foto)apparat, -e	camera
der	Freund, -e	friend; boyfriend
der	Jugendklub, -s	youth club
der	MP3-Spieler	MP3 player
der	Plattenspieler	record player
der	Sänger	singer
der	Schlager	hit (record)
der	Spaziergang, ⸚e	walk
der	Sport	sport
der	Tanz, ⸚e	dance
der	Verein, -e	club

ESSENTIAL WORDS *(feminine)*

die	Brieffreundin	penfriend
die	CD, -s	CD
die	Diskothek, -en	disco
die	DVD, -s	DVD
die	Einladung, -en	invitation
die	Eintrittskarte, -n	(admission) ticket
die	Fotografie, -n	photograph; photography
die	Freizeit	free time, spare time
die	Freundin	friend; girlfriend
die	Musik	music
die	Sängerin	singer
die	Spielekonsole, -n	games console
die	(Spiel)karte, -n	(playing) card
die	Stereoanlage, -en	stereo (system)
die	Zeitschrift, -en	magazine
die	Zeitung, -en	newspaper

ESSENTIAL WORDS *(neuter)*

das	**Fernsehen**	watching television
das	**Fitnessstudio, -s**	fitness centre
das	**Foto, -s**	photograph
das	**Hobby, -s**	hobby
das	**Interesse, -n**	interest
das	**Kartenspiel, -e**	game of cards; pack of cards
das	**Kino, -s**	cinema
das	**Kofferradio, -s**	transistor (radio)
das	**Konzert, -e**	concert
das	**Lesen**	reading
das	**Magazin, -e**	magazine
das	**Museum, Museen**	museum
das	**Programm, -e**	(TV) programme
das	**Radio, -s**	radio
das	**Singen**	singing
das	**Spiel, -e**	game
das	**Taschengeld**	pocket money
das	**Theater**	theatre
das	**Wandern**	hiking, rambling
das	**Wochenende, -n**	weekend

USEFUL PHRASES

in meiner Freizeit in my free *or* spare time
die Zeit damit verbringen, etw zu tun to spend time doing sth
am Wochenende at the weekend(s)
sich ausruhen to rest; beschließen to decide; treffen to meet
viel Spaß! enjoy yourself!, have fun!
es hat mir wirklich gut gefallen I really liked it
ausgezeichnet! excellent!; toll! terrific!
einen Spaziergang machen to go for a walk
fernsehen to watch television
Radio hören to listen to the radio
umschalten to turn over, change channels
CDs hören to play CDs; aufnehmen to record
fotografieren to take photos (of); knipsen to snap
lesen to read; schreiben to write; sammeln to collect
malen to paint; zeichnen to draw

IMPORTANT WORDS (*masculine*)

der	**Drachen**	kite; hang-glider
der	**Karneval, -e** *or* **-s**	carnival
der	**Krimi, -s**	thriller, detective story
der	**Pfadfinder**	boy scout
der	**Roman, -e**	novel
der	**Shoppingsender**	shopping channel
der	**Treffpunkt, -e**	meeting place
der	**Videorekorder**	video (recorder)
der	**Walkman®**	personal stereo, Walkman®
der	**Zoo, -s**	zoo

IMPORTANT WORDS (*feminine*)

die	**Aufnahme, -n**	shot (*photo*); recording
die	**Ausstellung, -en**	exhibition
die	**Besichtigung, -en**	visit
die	**(Briefmarken)sammlung, -en**	(stamp) collection
die	**Disko, -s**	disco
die	**Freizeitbeschäftigung, -en**	hobby, spare-time activity
die	**Illustrierte, -n**	magazine
die	**Musikkassette, -n**	music cassette
die	**Nachrichten** (*pl*)	news, newscast
die	**Pfadfinderin**	girl scout
die	**Sendung, -en**	transmission, programme
die	**Spielshow, -s**	game show
die	**Unterhaltung, -en**	entertainment; talk
die	**Verabredung, -en**	date, appointment
die	**Videokassette, -n**	video (cassette)
die	**Wanderung, -en**	walk, hike

IMPORTANT WORDS (*neuter*)

das	**Dia, -s**	slide, transparency
das	**Mitglied, -er**	member
das	**Schach**	chess
das	**Taschenbuch, ⸚er**	paperback

USEFUL WORDS (masculine)

der	CD-Spieler	CD player
das	Chatraum, -räume	chatroom
die	Comics (pl)	cartoons, comic strips
der	Feierabend, -e	end of work, evening
der	Ohrstöpsel	earplug
der	Spielautomat, -en	slot machine
der	Zeitvertreib, -e	pastime

USEFUL WORDS (feminine)

die	CD, -s, die Compactdisc, -s	compact disc, CD
die	Fernsehsendung, -en	TV programme
die	Filmkamera, -s	cine camera
die	Freizeitdroge, -n	recreational drug
die	Hitliste, -n	charts, top twenty
die	Hitparade, -en	charts, hit parade
die	Party, -s	party
die	Versammlung, -en	meeting, gathering

USEFUL WORDS (neuter)

das	Album, Alben	album
das	Damespiel	draughts
das	Feriendorf, ⁻er	holiday camp
das	Ferienlager	school camp
das	Freizeitzentrum, -zentren	leisure centre
das	Gleitschirmfliegen	paragliding
das	Jugendzentrum, -zentren	youth centre
das	Kegeln	bowling
das	Kreuzworträtsel	crossword (puzzle)
das	Lied, -er	song
das	Skateboard, -s	skateboard
das	Snowboard, -s	snowboard
das	Surfen	surfing

USEFUL PHRASES

ich interessiere mich für (+ acc) I am interested in ...
eine Party geben to have a party
hast du Lust, zu meiner Party zu kommen? do you fancy coming to my party?

ESSENTIAL + IMPORTANT WORDS (masculine)

der	Apfel, ¨	apple
der	Apfelbaum, -bäume	apple tree
der	Birnbaum, -bäume	pear tree
der	Obstbaum, -bäume	fruit tree
der	Obstgarten, ¨	orchard
der	Pfirsich, -e	peach
der	Pfirsichbaum, -bäume	peach tree
der	Weinstock, ¨e	vine

ESSENTIAL + IMPORTANT WORDS (feminine)

die	Apfelsine, -n	orange
die	Banane, -n	banana; banana tree
die	Birne, -n	pear
die	Erdbeere, -n	strawberry
eine	Frucht, ¨e	a (piece of) fruit
die	Himbeere, -n	raspberry
die	Kirsche, -n	cherry
die	Melone, -n	melon
die	Olive, -n	olive
die	Orange, -n	orange; orange tree
die	Pflaume, -n	plum
die	Schale, -n	skin; peel; shell
die	(Wein)traube, -n	grape; bunch of grapes
die	Zitrone, -n	lemon

ESSENTIAL WORDS (neuter)

das	Kompott, -e	stewed fruit
das	Obst	fruit
das	Stück Obst	piece of fruit

USEFUL PHRASES

reif ripe; unreif not ripe; süß sweet; bitter sour, bitter
hart hard; weich soft; saftig juicy
pflücken to pick; sammeln to gather
essen to eat; beißen to bite
blaue/grüne Trauben black/green grapes

USEFUL WORDS (masculine)

der	Granatapfel, ⁻	pomegranate
der	Kern, -e	pip, stone (in fruit)
der	Nussbaum, -bäume	walnut tree
der	Rhabarber	rhubarb
der	Walnussbaum, -bäume	walnut tree
der	Weinberg, -e	vineyard
der	Weinstock, ⁻e	vine

USEFUL WORDS (feminine)

die	Ananas, - or -se	pineapple
die	Aprikose, -n	apricot; apricot tree
die	Backpflaume, -n	prune
die	Beere, -n	berry
die	Brombeere, -n	blackberry, bramble
die	Dattel, -n	date
die	Erdnuss, ⁻e	peanut
die	Feige, -n	fig
die	Grapefruit	grapefruit
die	Haselnuss, ⁻e	hazelnut
die	Heidelbeere, -n	bilberry
die	Johannisbeere, -n	redcurrant
die	Schwarze Johannisbeere, -n -n	blackcurrant
die	Kastanie, -n	chestnut; chestnut tree
die	Kiwi, -s	kiwi (fruit)
die	Kokosnuss, ⁻e	coconut
die	Mandarine, -n	tangerine
die	Nuss, ⁻e	nut
die	Pampelmuse, -n	grapefruit
die	Passionsfrucht, ⁻e	passion fruit
die	Stachelbeere, -n	gooseberry
die	Traube, -n	grape; bunch of grapes
die	Traubenlese	grape harvest, vintage
die	Walnuss, ⁻e	walnut
die	(Wein)rebe, -n	vine
die	Zwetsch(g)e, -n	plum

ESSENTIAL WORDS *(masculine)*

der	Fernsehapparat, -e *or*	television set
	der Fernseher	
der	Herd, -e	cooker
der	Kleiderschrank, ¨e	wardrobe
der	Kühlschrank, ¨e	fridge, refrigerator
der	Plattenspieler	record player
der	Raum, Räume	room
der	Satellitenempfänger	satellite receiver
der	Schrank, ¨e	cupboard
der	Sessel	armchair
der	Stuhl, ¨e	chair
der	Tisch, -e	table
der	Wecker	alarm clock

ESSENTIAL WORDS *(feminine)*

die	Lampe, -n	lamp
die	Stehlampe, -n	standard lamp, floor lamp
die	Stereoanlage, -n	stereo system
die	Uhr, -en	clock
die	Waschmaschine, -n	washing machine

ESSENTIAL WORDS *(neuter)*

das	Bett, -en	bed
das	Bild, -er	picture, painting
das	Haus, Häuser	house
das	Sofa, -s	settee, couch
das	Telefon, -e	telephone
das	Zimmer	room

USEFUL PHRASES

fernsehen to watch television; im Fernsehen on television
telefonieren to telephone; anrufen to phone, call
Musik hören to listen to music
programmieren to program

IMPORTANT WORDS *(masculine)*

der **CD-Brenner**	CD burner
der **CD-Spieler**	CD player
der **DVD-Brenner**	DVD burner
der **DVD-Spieler**	DVD player
der **Elektroherd, -e**	electric cooker
der **Gasherd, -e**	gas cooker
der **Nachttisch, -e**	bedside table
der **Ofen, ∵**	oven
der **Spiegel**	mirror
der **Videorekorder**	video recorder

IMPORTANT WORDS *(feminine)*

die **Digicam, -s**	digicam
die **Schreibmaschine, -n**	typewriter
die **Spülmaschine, -n**	dishwasher
die **Steckdose, -n**	(wall) socket

IMPORTANT WORDS *(neuter)*

das **(Bücher)regal, -e**	bookcase, bookshelves
ein **digitales Radio, -n -s**	digital radio
das **Fax, -e**	fax
das **Handy, -s**	mobile phone
die **Möbel** *(pl)*	furniture
das **Möbel(stück)**	piece of furniture
das **Regal, -e**	(set of) shelves
das **Videogerät, -e**	video (recorder)
das **Walkman®**	personal stereo, Walkman®

USEFUL PHRASES

ein Zimmer möblieren **to furnish a room**
ein möbliertes Zimmer **a furnished room**
bequem **comfortable**; unbequem **uncomfortable**
in dem Zimmer ist es sehr eng **the room is very cramped**
den Tisch decken/abräumen **to lay** *or* **set/to clear the table**
das Bett machen **to make the bed**
ins Bett gehen, zu Bett gehen **to go to bed**

USEFUL WORDS (*masculine*)

der	**Anrufbeantworter**	answering machine
der	**Backofen, ⸚**	oven
der	**Beamer**	data projector
der	**Bücherschrank, ⸚e**	bookcase
der	**Couchtisch, -e**	coffee table
der	**Esstisch, -e**	dining table
der	**Frisiertisch, -e**	dressing table
der	**Heizofen, ⸚**	fire, heater
der	**Hocker**	stool
der	**Kabelanschluss, ⸚e**	cable connection
der	**Lehnsessel** *or* der **Lehnstuhl, ⸚e**	armchair
der	**Mikrowellenherd, -e**	microwave oven
der	**Möbelwagen**	furniture van, removal van
der	**Nachtspeicherofen**	(night-)storage heater
der	**Radiowecker**	radio alarm clock
der	**Satz (⸚e) Tische**	nest of tables
der	**Schaukelstuhl, ⸚e**	rocking chair
der	**Schirmständer**	umbrella stand
der	**Schnellkochtopf, ⸚e**	pressure cooker
der	**Schreibtisch, -e**	writing desk
der	**Sekretär, -e**	bureau, writing desk
der	**Staubsauger**	vacuum cleaner, Hoover®
der	**Teewagen**	trolley
der	**Umluftherd, -e**	fan-assisted oven
der	**Umzug, ⸚e**	removal
der	**Wäschetrockner**	tumble dryer

USEFUL PHRASES

sitzen to sit, be sitting; sich setzen to sit down
sich hinlegen to lie down; sich ausruhen to rest
ein Zimmer ausräumen to clear out a room
ein Zimmer aufräumen *or* in Ordnung bringen to tidy up a room
putzen to clean; abstauben to dust; staubsaugen to hoover

USEFUL WORDS *(feminine)*

die **Anrichte, -n**	dresser; sideboard
die **Antenne, -n**	aerial
die **Einrichtung**	furnishings *(pl)*
die **Fernbedienung, -en**	remote control
die **Gefriertruhe, -n**	freezer
die **Kommode, -n**	chest of drawers
die **Matratze, -n**	mattress
die **Nähmaschine, -n**	sewing machine
die **Satellitenantenne, -n**	satellite dish
die **Schublade, -n**	drawer
die **Spedition, -en**	removal firm
die **Standuhr, -en**	grandfather clock
die **Tiefkühltruhe, -n**	freezer, deep freeze
die **Truhe, -n**	chest, trunk
die **Videokamera, -s**	video camera
die **Wäscheschleuder, -n**	spin dryer
die **Waage, -n**	(bathroom) scales
die **Wiege, -n**	cradle

USEFUL WORDS *(neuter)*

das **Bord, -e**	shelf
das **Etagenbett, -en**	bunk bed
das **Gemälde**	painting, picture
das **Gerät, -e**	appliance
das **Kinderbettchen**	cot
das **Rollo, -s** *or* das **Rouleau, -s**	blind
das **Schubfach, ‑er**	drawer
ein **schnurlose Telefon, -n -e**	cordless telephone
das **Tonbandgerät, -e**	tape recorder

USEFUL PHRASES

elektrisch electric; **anmachen, einschalten** to turn *or* switch on
ausmachen, ausschalten to turn *or* switch off
es funktioniert nicht it's not working
heizen to heat; **gemütlich** comfortable, cosy

die	Alpen (pl)	the Alps
	Antwerpen (nt)	Antwerp
der	Ärmelkanal	the English Channel
der	Atlantik,	the Atlantic (Ocean)
der	Atlantische Ozean	
	Basel (nt)	Basle
	Bayern (nt)	Bavaria
	Berlin (nt)	Berlin
der	Bodensee	Lake Constance
die	Britischen Inseln (fpl)	the British Isles
	Brüssel (nt)	Brussels
die	Donau	the Danube
	Edinburg (nt)	Edinburgh
die	Elbe	the (river) Elbe
das	Elsass (nt)	Alsace
der	Ferne Osten	the Far East
	Genf (nt)	Geneva
der	Genfer See	Lake Geneva
	Gent (nt)	Ghent
Den	Haag (nt)	The Hague
	Hannover (nt)	Hanover
	Kairo (nt)	Cairo
die	Kanalinseln (fpl)	the Channel Islands
	Köln (nt)	Cologne
	Korsika (nt)	Corsica
	Lissabon (nt)	Lisbon
	Lothringen (nt)	Lorraine
	Mailand (nt)	Milan
	Mallorca (nt)	Majorca
das	Mittelmeer	the Mediterranean
die	Mosel	Moselle
	Moskau (nt)	Moscow
	München (nt)	Munich
der	Nahe Osten	the Middle East
die	Nordsee	the North Sea
die	Ostsee	the Baltic Sea
der	Pazifik,	the Pacific (Ocean)
der	Pazifische Ozean	
	Peking (nt)	Beijing
die	Pyrenäen (pl)	the Pyrenees

der	**Rhein**	the Rhine
	Rom *(nt)*	Rome
der	**Schwarzwald**	the Black Forest
die	**Seine**	the Seine
der	**Stille Ozean**	the Pacific Ocean
die	**Themse**	the Thames
	Venedig *(nt)*	Venice
der	**Vesuv**	Mount Vesuvius
	Warschau *(nt)*	Warsaw
	Wien *(nt)*	Vienna
die	**Wolga**	the Volga

USEFUL PHRASES

Athener, -in an Athenian
Bas(e)ler, -in a person from Basle
Bayer, -in a Bavarian
Böhme, Böhmin a person from Bohemia
Elsässer, -in a person from Alsace, an Alsatian
Flame, Flamin *or* Flämin a person from Flanders, a Fleming
Friese, Friesin a person from Frisia, a Frisian
Hamburger, -in a person from Hamburg
Hannoveraner, -in a person from Hanover, a Hanoverian
Hesse, Hessin a person from Hesse
Indianer, -in an (American) Indian
Londoner, -in a Londoner
Moskauer, -in a person from Moscow, a Muscovite
Münch(e)ner, -in a person from Munich
Neapolitaner, -in a Neapolitan
Pariser, -in a Parisian
Preuße, Preußin a Prussian
Rheinländer, -in a Rheinlander
Römer, -in a person from Rome, a Roman
Sachse, Sächsin a person from Saxony
Schwabe, Schwäbin a person from Swabia
Tiroler, -in a person from the Tyrol
Venezianer, -in a Venetian
Westfale, Westfälin a Westphalian
Wiener, -in a person from Vienna, a Viennese

GREETINGS AND FAREWELLS

guten Tag! good day, hello; good afternoon
guten Morgen! good morning
guten Abend! good evening
gute Nacht! good night *(when going to bed)*
auf Wiedersehen! goodbye
auf Wiederhören! goodbye *(on phone)*
hallo! hi!; **tschüss!** bye!; **servus** hello; goodbye
grüß Gott! hello
wie geht's?; wie geht es Ihnen? how are things?
gut, danke; es geht mir gut, danke very well, thank you
sehr angenehm pleased to meet you
bis später see you later
bis morgen see you tomorrow

BEST WISHES

ich gratuliere! congratulations!
alles Gute all the best, best wishes
herzlichen Glückwunsch congratulations, best wishes
alles Gute zum Geburtstag happy birthday
alles Gute zum Hochzeitstag congratulations on your wedding day
viel Glück all the best; the best of luck
machs gut! take care
fröhliche Weihnachten merry Christmas
gutes neues Jahr happy New Year
guten Appetit! have a good meal, enjoy your meal
prost! cheers; **zum Wohl!** good health!
Gesundheit! bless you! *(after a sneeze)*
viel Spaß! have a good time, enjoy yourself *etc*
schlaf gut! sleep well
gut geschlafen? did you sleep well?

grüßen, begrüßen to greet, welcome
sich verabschieden to say goodbye, take one's leave
(sich) vorstellen to introduce (oneself)

SURPRISE

ach du meine Güte oh my goodness, oh dear
so?, wirklich? really?
so, so! well, well!; **ach so!** oh I see!
na, so etwas! you don't say!
wie? what?
was für ein Glück! what a piece of luck!

POLITENESS

bitte please, excuse me
danke thank you; **nein danke** no thank you
ja bitte, bitte ja yes please
tu das ja nicht don't do that
danke schön, danke sehr, vielen Dank thank you very much, many thanks
nichts zu danken don't mention it
bitte schön, bitte sehr don't mention it
gern geschehen my pleasure, don't mention it
entschuldigen Sie, Entschuldigung excuse me, I'm sorry
verzeihen Sie, Verzeihung I'm sorry, I beg your pardon
pardon excuse me, I'm sorry
das macht nichts it doesn't matter
(wie) bitte? (I beg your) pardon?
hier bitte, bitte schön, bitte sehr there you are
mit Vergnügen with pleasure
machen Sie keine Umstände don't go to any trouble

WARNINGS

Achtung! watch out!; **Vorsicht!** be careful!
pass auf! look out!, watch out!
halten Sie! stop!
Feuer! fire!; **haltet den Dieb!** stop thief!
Ruhe!, ruhig! be quiet!; **halt den Mund!** shut up!
herein! come in!; **hinaus!** get out!
beeile dich! hurry up!; **hau ab!** clear off!
geh mir aus dem Weg! get out of my way!

AGREEMENT AND DISAGREEMENT

ja yes; **doch** yes *(when contradictory)*
nein no
jawohl yes indeed
natürlich of course
natürlich nicht, aber nein of course not
nicht wahr? isn't that right?
in Ordnung O.K., all right
gut good, O.K.
na gut, also gut O.K. then, all right then
schön fine
einverstanden! agreed!
genau, ganz recht exactly
desto besser so much the better
ich habe nichts dagegen I don't mind *or* object
das ist mir gleich *or* **einerlei** *or* **egal** I don't mind, it's all the same to me, it's all one to me
das stimmt that's right
das stimmt nicht that doesn't make sense
im Gegenteil on the contrary
nie!, um nichts in der Welt! never!, not on your life!
kümmern Sie sich um Ihre eigenen Dinge! mind your own business!
nieder mit ... down with ...

DISTRESS

Hilfe! help!
ach je! oh dear!
ach!, o weh! alas!
was ist los (mit dir)? what's the matter (with you)?, what's wrong
  (with you)?
leider (nicht) unfortunately (not)
es tut mir Leid I'm sorry
es tut mir wirklich Leid I'm really sorry
wie schade what a pity
das ist Pech it's a shame, that's bad luck
verflixt (noch mal)! blow!, drat!, dash it!
verflucht!, verdammt! damn!
ich habe es satt I'm fed up with it
ich kann ihn nicht ausstehen I can't stand him
was soll ich tun? what shall I do?
wie ärgerlich! what a nuisance!, how annoying!

OTHER EXPRESSIONS

vielleicht perhaps, maybe
ich weiß nicht I don't know
(ich habe) keine Ahnung (I've) no idea
ich weiß da nicht Bescheid I don't know (anything about it)
ich weiß nicht genau I don't know exactly
das kann ich mir vorstellen I can believe that
schade! shame!
mein Gott! good Lord!
(ach) du lieber Himmel! (good) heavens!, goodness gracious!
prima! great!
klasse! terrific!, marvellous!
machen Sie sich keine Sorgen don't worry
aber wirklich! well really!
du machst wohl Witze you must be joking *or* kidding!
so eine Frechheit! what a nerve *or* cheek!
armes Ding! poor thing!

ESSENTIAL WORDS (masculine)

der Arzt, ∺e	doctor, G.P.
der Durchfall	diarrhoea
die Kopfschmerzen (pl)	a headache
Kranke(r), -n	patient
der Krankenwagen	ambulance
der Zahnarzt, ∺e	dentist

ESSENTIAL WORDS (feminine)

die Allergie, -n	allergy
die Ärztin	doctor, G.P.
die Erkältung, -en	cold; chill
die erste Hilfe	first aid
die Gesundheit	health
die Grippe	flu, influenza
die Klinik, -en	hospital, clinic
die Krankenschwester, -n	nurse
die Krankheit, -en	illness
die Lebensgefahr	danger (to life)
die Medizin	(science of) medicine
die Pille, -n	pill
die Tablette, -n	tablet, pill
die Temperatur, -en	temperature
die Verstopfung, -en	constipation

ESSENTIAL WORDS (neuter)

das Fieber	fever, (high) temperature
das Heimweh	homesickness
das Kopfweh	headache
das Krankenhaus, -häuser	hospital

USEFUL PHRASES

krank ill; gesund healthy; wohl well
schwach weak; atemlos breathless
müde tired; schwindlig dizzy; blass pale
sich erkälten to catch cold; erkältet sein to have a cold
husten to cough; niesen to sneeze; schwitzen to sweat

IMPORTANT WORDS (masculine)

der	**Apotheker**	(dispensing) chemist
der	**Atem**	breath
der	**Auslandskrankenschein, -e**	(European) health insurance card
die	**Bauchschmerzen** (pl)	stomach-ache
der	**Gips**	plaster; plaster of Paris
die	**Halsschmerzen** (pl)	a sore throat
der	**Husten**	cough
der	**Krankenpfleger**	(male) nurse
der	**Krankenschein, -e**	health insurance card
der	**Krebs**	cancer
die	**Magenschmerzen** (pl)	stomach-ache
der	**Operationssaal, -säle**	operating theatre
der	**Patient, -en**	patient
der	**Schmerz, -en**	pain, ache
der	**Schnupfen**	cold (in the head)
der	**Schweiß**	sweat
der	**Sonnenbrand, ̈-e**	sunburn
der	**Tod, -e**	death
der	**Tropfen**	drop
der	**Verband, ̈-e**	bandage, dressing
die	**Zahnschmerzen** (pl)	toothache

IMPORTANT WORDS (feminine)

die	**Behandlung**	treatment
die	**Feuerwehr, -en**	fire brigade
die	**Krankenkasse, -n**	health insurance
die	**Kur, -en**	health cure
die	**Operation, -en**	operation
die	**Patientin**	patient
die	**Ruhe**	rest
die	**Sorge, -n**	care, worry
die	**Spritze, -n**	syringe; injection
die	**Untersuchung, -en**	medical examination
die	**Verletzung, -en**	injury
die	**Versichertenkarte, -n**	health insurance card
die	**Wunde, -n**	wound

IMPORTANT WORDS (neuter)

das	Aids	AIDS, aids
das	Aspirin	aspirin
das	Blut	blood
das	Heftpflaster	sticking plaster
das	Kondom, -e	condom
das	Medikament, -e	medicine
das	Rezept, -e	prescription
das	Thermometer	thermometer
das	Verhütungsmittel	contraceptive

USEFUL WORDS (feminine)

die	Abmagerungskur, -en	(slimming) diet
die	Akne	acne
die	Blase, -n	blister; bladder
die	Blinddarmentzündung, -en	appendicitis
die	Blutübertragung, -en	blood transfusion
die	Chemotherapie, -n	chemotherapy
die	Diät, -en	(special) diet
die	Droge, -n	drug
die	Epidemie, -n	epidemic
die	Genesung	recovery
die	Kraft, ¨e	strength, power
die	Magenverstimmung	stomach upset
die	Mandelentzündung	tonsillitis
die	Masern (pl)	measles
die	Migräne	migraine
die	Narbe, -n	scar
die	Poliklinik, -en	health centre
die	Röntgenaufnahme, -n	X-ray
die	Röteln (pl)	German measles
die	Salbe, -n	ointment, cream
die	Schwangerschaft, -en	pregnancy
die	Station, -en	ward
die	Übelkeit	sickness, vomiting
die	Watte	cotton wool
die	Windpocken (pl)	chickenpox

USEFUL WORDS (masculine)

der	Bazillus, Bazillen	germ
der	blaue Fleck, -n -en	bruise
der	Blutdruck	blood pressure
der	Drogenmissbrauch	drug abuse
der	Fußpilz	athlete's foot
der	Heuschnupfen	hayfever
	HIV-Infizierte(r), -n	person who is HIV-positive
der	Kratzer	scratch
der	Mumps	mumps
der	Puls	pulse
der	Rollstuhl, ⁻e	wheelchair
der	Schlaganfall, ⁻e	stroke
der	Schock, -s	shock
der	Sonnenstich, -e	sunstroke
der	Stress	stress
der	Stich, -e	sting

USEFUL WORDS (neuter)

das	Altersheim, -e	old people's home
das	Antibiotikum, -ka	antibiotic
das	Gift, -e	poison
das	Rauschgift, -e	drug, narcotic
das	Sprechzimmer	surgery, consulting room
das	Wartezimmer	waiting room

USEFUL PHRASES

fallen, stürzen to fall; brechen to break
ich bin mit dem Auto verunglückt I've had an accident with the car
was fehlt Ihnen? what's the matter with you?
es blutet it's bleeding; es tut weh it hurts
verletzt injured, hurt; verwundet wounded
sich übergeben to vomit, be sick
untersuchen to examine; verbinden to bandage
pflegen to look after, nurse; behandeln to treat
verschreiben to prescribe; gute Besserung! get well soon!
sich erholen to recover; sterben to die; tot dead

ESSENTIAL WORDS *(masculine)*

der	(Farb)fernseher	(colour) television set
der	Gast, ⸚e	guest
der	Gasthof, ⸚e	hotel, inn
der	Kellner	waiter
der	Koch, ⸚e	cook
der	Koffer	case, suitcase
der	Lift, -e *or* -s	lift
der	Notausgang, ⸚e	emergency exit
der	Reisepass, ⸚e	passport
der	Schalter	switch
der	Scheck, -s	cheque
der	Schlüssel	key
der	Stock, Stockwerke	floor, storey
der	Tag, -e	day
der	Weinkellner	wine waiter
der	Zuschlag, ⸚e	extra charge

ESSENTIAL WORDS *(feminine)*

die	Anmeldung	registration
die	Antwort, -en	answer
die	Bar, -s	bar
die	Bedienung	service; service charge
die	Dusche, -n	shower
die	Halbpension	half board
die	Kellnerin	waitress
die	Köchin	cook
die	Mahlzeit, -en	meal
die	Nacht, ⸚e	night
die	Pension, -en	guest-house, boarding house
die	Rechnung, -en	bill
die	Tasche, -n	bag
die	Toilette, -n	toilet
die	Übernachtung mit Frühstück	bed and breakfast
die	Vollpension	full board
die	Woche, -n	week

ESSENTIAL + IMPORTANT WORDS *(neuter)*

das	**Badezimmer**	bathroom
das	**Café, -s**	café
das	**Doppelbett, -en**	double bed
das	**Doppelzimmer**	double room
das	**Einzelzimmer**	single room
das	**Erdgeschoss, -e**	ground floor, ground level
das	**(Farb)fernsehen**	(colour) television
das	**Formular, -e**	form
das	**Freibad, -̈er**	open-air swimming pool
das	**Fremdenzimmer**	guest room
das	**Frühstück, -e**	breakfast
das	**Gasthaus, -häuser**	inn, hotel
das	**Gepäck**	luggage
das	**Hotel, -s**	hotel
das	**Kleingeld**	small change
das	**Mittagessen**	lunch
das	**Restaurant, -s**	restaurant
das	**Speisezimmer**	dining room
das	**(Tele)fax, -e**	fax
das	**Telefon, -e**	telephone
das	**Treppenhaus, -häuser**	staircase
das	**Wirtshaus, -häuser**	inn
das	**Zimmer**	room
das	**Zimmermädchen**	chambermaid

USEFUL PHRASES

einpacken to get packed; auspacken to get unpacked
ich habe schon gebucht I have already booked
eine Reservierung bestätigen to confirm a reservation
sich in einem Hotel anmelden to book in at a hotel
ich möchte hier übernachten I'd like a room for the night here
ein Formular ausfüllen to fill in a form
3 Tage bleiben to stay for 3 days

IMPORTANT WORDS (masculine)

der	Aufenthalt, -e	stay
der	Aufzug, -̈e	lift
der	Balkon, -s or -e	balcony
der	Blick, -e	view
der	Empfangschef, -s	receptionist, reception clerk
der	Feuerlöscher	fire extinguisher
der	Gepäckträger	porter
der	Hotelier, -s	hotelier, hotel-keeper
der	Mehrwertsteuer	value added tax
der	Prospekt, -e	leaflet, brochure
der	Reiseführer	guide-book; travel guide (person)
der	Reiseleiter	travel courier
der	Stern, -e	star

IMPORTANT WORDS (feminine)

die	Aussicht, -en	view
die	Empfangsdame, -n	receptionist
die	Garderobe, -n	cloakroom
die	Gaststätte, -n	restaurant; pub
die	Kneipe, -n	pub
die	Nummer, -n	number
die	Rezeption, -en	reception, reception desk
die	Terrasse, -n	terrace
die	Unterkunft, -künfte	accommodation
die	Veranstaltung, -en	organization

USEFUL WORDS (masculine)

der	**Brand, ⁻e**	fire
der	**(Gast)wirt, -e**	owner, innkeeper, landlord
der	**Ober**	waiter
der	**Oberkellner**	head waiter

USEFUL WORDS (feminine)

die	**(Gast)wirtin**	owner, innkeeper, landlady
die	**Vorhalle, -n**	foyer

USEFUL WORDS (neuter)

das	**Foyer**	foyer
das	**Kellergeschoss, -e**	basement
das	**Schwimmbecken**	swimming pool
das	**Stockwerk, -e**	floor, storey
das	**Trinkgeld, -er**	tip
das	**Wechselgeld**	change
das	**Zweibettzimmer**	twin-bedded room

USEFUL PHRASES

ich möchte ein Zimmer mit Dusche/mit Bad I'd like a room with
a shower/with a bath

was kostet es?, wie teuer ist es? how much is it?

das ist ziemlich teuer that is rather expensive

das Zimmer hat Aussicht *or* Blick auf den Strand the room overlooks the
beach

im ersten/zehnten Stock on the first/tenth floor

im Erdgeschoss on the ground floor, on ground level

Herr Ober! waiter!

Fräulein! excuse me, miss!

„Bedienung inbegriffen" "service included"

„inklusive Bedienung" "inclusive of service"

„Sie brauchen nur zu klingeln" "just ring"

„Zimmer frei" "vacancies"

ESSENTIAL WORDS (masculine)

der **Bungalow, -s**	bungalow
der **Flur, -e**	(entrance) hall
der **(Fuß)boden,** ⸚	floor
der **Garten,** ⸚	garden
der **Haushalt**	household
der **Hof,** ⸚e	yard
der **Keller**	cellar
der **Mieter**	tenant
der **Park, -s**	public park
der **Parkplatz,** ⸚e	parking space
der **Raum, Räume**	room; space
der **Schlüssel**	key
der **Speisesaal, -säle**	dining room
der **Stein, -e**	stone
der **Stock, Stockwerke**	floor, storey

ESSENTIAL WORDS (feminine)

die **Adresse, -n**	address
die **Dusche, -n**	shower
die **Familie, -n**	family
die **Garage, -n**	garage
die **Hausfrau, -en**	housewife
die **Haustür, -en**	front door
die **Küche, -n**	kitchen; cooking
die **Miete, -n**	rent
die **Stadt,** ⸚e	town
die **Straße, -n**	street, road
die **Toilette, -n**	toilet
die **Treppe, -n**	stairs, staircase
die **Tür, -en**	door
die **Wand,** ⸚e	(inside) wall
die **Wohnung, -en**	flat

USEFUL PHRASES

in der Stadt/auf dem Lande wohnen to live in the town/in the country
mieten to rent; bauen to build; besitzen to own

ESSENTIAL WORDS (neuter)

das	Bad, ¨-er; das Badezimmer	bathroom
das	Doppelhaus, -häuser	semi-detached (house)
das	Dorf, ¨-er	village
das	Einfamilienhaus, -häuser	detached house
das	Erdgeschoss, -e	ground floor, ground level
das	Esszimmer	dining room
das	Fenster	window
das	Haus, Häuser	house
das	Klo, das Klosett	toilet, loo
das	Reihenhaus, -häuser	terraced house
das	Schlafzimmer	bedroom
das	Schloss, ¨-er	lock
das	Treppenhaus	staircase
das	Wohnzimmer	lounge, living room
das	Zentrum, Zentren	centre
das	Zimmer	room

IMPORTANT WORDS (neuter)

das	Dach, ¨-er	roof
das	Gebäude	building
das	Gebiet, -e	area
das	Hochhaus, -häuser	high-rise (building)
die	Möbel (pl)	furniture
das	Möbel(stück)	piece of furniture
das	Parkett, -e	wooden or parquet floor
das	Tor, -e	gate

USEFUL WORDS (neuter)

das	Arbeitszimmer	study
das	Dachfenster	skylight
das	Gästezimmer	spare room, guest room
das	Kellergeschoss, -e	basement
das	Oberlicht, -er	skylight
das	Stockwerk, -e	floor, storey

IMPORTANT WORDS *(masculine)*

der **Aufzug**, ⁻e	lift
der **Balkon**, -s *or* -e	balcony
der **Bezirk**, -e	district
der **Dachboden**, ⁻	attic, loft
der **Einwohner**	inhabitant
der **Gang**, ⁻e	corridor
der **Kamin**, -e	chimney; fireplace
der **Landkreis**, -e	region
der **Nachbar**, -n	neighbour
der **Rasen**	lawn; grass
der **Vorort**, -e	suburb

IMPORTANT WORDS *(feminine)*

die **Anlage**, -n	layout
die **Aussicht**, -en	view
die **Decke**, -n	ceiling
die **Gegend**, -en	district, area
die **Kohle**, -n	coal
die **Lage**, -n	position, situation
die **Mauer**, -n	(*outside*) wall
die **Nachbarin**	neighbour
die **Telefonnummer**, -n	phone number
die **Terrasse**, -n	patio
die **Türklingel**, -n	doorbell
die **Umgebung**, -en	surroundings (*pl*)
die **Zentralheizung**, -en	central heating

USEFUL PHRASES

es klopft **somebody's knocking at the door**
es klingelt **somebody's ringing the doorbell**
im ersten/dritten Stock **on the first/third floor**
im Erdgeschoss **on the ground floor, on ground level**
oben **upstairs**; unten **downstairs**
zu Hause, daheim **at home**
umziehen **to move (house)**; einziehen **to move in**
sich einleben **to settle down, settle in**

USEFUL WORDS *(masculine)*

der	Besitzer	owner
der	(Fenster)laden, ¨e	shutter
der *or* das	(Fenster)sims, -e	window sill *or* ledge
der	Hausmeister	caretaker
der	Hauswirt, -e	landlord
der *or* das	Kaminsims, -e	mantelpiece
der	Korridor, -e	corridor
der	Rauch	smoke
der	Schornstein, -e	chimney
der	(Treppen)absatz, ¨e	landing
der	Umzug, ¨e	removal
der	Wintergarten, ¨	conservatory
der	Wohnblock, -s	block of flats
der	Zaun, Zäune	fence

USEFUL WORDS *(feminine)*

die	Allee, -n	avenue
die	Antenne, -n	aerial
die	Einrichtung, -en	furnishings *(pl)*
die	Etagenwohnung, -en	flat
die	Fensterscheibe, -n	window pane
die	Fliese, -n	tile
die	Gasse, -n	lane *(in town)*
die	Hecke, -n	hedge
die	Jalousie, -n	venetian blind
die	Kachel, -n	(wall) tile
die	Kellerwohnung, -en	basement flat
die	Mansarde, -n	attic
die	Putzfrau, -en	cleaner
die	Rumpelkammer, -n	box room, junk room
die	Stube, -n	room
die	(Tür)stufe, -n	(door)step
die	Verandatür, -en	French window
die	(Wohn)siedlung, -en	housing estate

ESSENTIAL WORDS *(masculine)*

der **Briefkasten, ⸚**	letterbox
der **Fernsehapparat, -e** *or* der **Fernseher**	television set
der **Föhn, -e**	hair-drier
der **Knopf, ⸚e**	knob, button
der **Kühlschrank, ⸚e**	fridge
der **Schalter**	switch
der **Schrank, ⸚e**	cupboard
der **Topf, ⸚e**	pot
der **Wecker**	alarm clock

ESSENTIAL WORDS *(feminine)*

die **Bürste, -n**	brush
die **Dusche, -n**	shower
die **Farbe, -n**	paint; colour
die **Gardine, -n**	curtain
die **Hausarbeit**	housework
die **Kanne, -n**	jug; pot
die **Lampe, -n**	lamp
die **Sachen** *(pl)*	things
die **Seife**	soap
die **Zahnbürste, -n**	toothbrush
die **Zahncreme, -s** *or* die **Zahnpasta, -pasten**	toothpaste

ESSENTIAL WORDS *(neuter)*

das **Bild, -er**	picture, painting
das **Handtuch, ⸚er**	towel
das **Licht, -er**	light
das **Poster**	poster
das **Wasser**	water

USEFUL PHRASES

die Hausarbeit machen to do the housework
duschen to have a shower; baden to have a bath

IMPORTANT WORDS *(masculine)*

der	**Abfall, ̈-e**	rubbish, refuse
der	**Abfalleimer**	rubbish bin
der	**Aschenbecher**	ashtray
der	**Haartrockner**	hair-drier
der	**Kamm, ̈-e**	comb
der	**Rasierapparat, -e**	razor
der	**Spiegel**	mirror
der	**Teppich, -e**	carpet
der	**Vorhang, ̈-e**	curtain
der	**(Wasser)hahn, ̈-e**	tap

IMPORTANT WORDS *(feminine)*

die	**(Bade)wanne, -n**	bath
die	**(Bett)decke, -n**	blanket, cover
die	**Bettwäsche**	bed linen
die	**Birne, -n**	(light) bulb
die	**Bratpfanne, -n**	frying pan
die	**Elektrizität**	electricity
die	**Kerze, -n**	candle

IMPORTANT WORDS *(neuter)*

das	**Federbett, -en**	continental quilt
das	**Feuer**	fire
das	**Gas**	gas
das	**Geschirr**	crockery; pots and pans
das	**Kissen**	cushion; pillow
das	**Kopfkissen**	pillow
das	**Putzen**	cleaning
das	**Rezept, -e**	recipe
das	**Shampoo, -s**	shampoo
das	**Spülbecken**	sink
das	**Tablett, -e**	tray
das	**Waschbecken**	washbasin

USEFUL WORDS (masculine)

der **Besen**	broom
der **Bettvorleger**	bedside rug
der **Dampfkochtopf, ⁻e**	pressure cooker
der **Deckel**	lid
der **Eimer**	bucket
der **Griff, -e**	handle (of door etc)
der **Handbesen** or der **Handfeger**	brush
der **Heizkörper**	radiator
der **Henkel**	handle (of jug etc)
der **Kachelofen, ⁻**	tiled stove
der **Kessel**	kettle
der **Kleiderbügel**	coat hanger
der **Krug, ⁻e**	jug
der **Mixer**	(electric) blender
der **Müll**	rubbish, refuse
der **Mülleimer**	dustbin
der **Papierkorb, ⁻e**	waste paper basket
der **Pinsel**	paintbrush; brush
der **Rasierpinsel**	shaving brush
der **Schmutz**	dirt
der **Schneebesen**	whisk, egg beater
der **Schwamm, ⁻e**	sponge
der **Staub**	dust
der **Staubsauger**	vacuum cleaner, Hoover®
der **Teppichboden, ⁻**	fitted carpet
der **Toaster**	toaster
der **Ziergegenstand, ⁻e**	ornament

USEFUL PHRASES

sein eigenes Zimmer haben **to have a room of one's own**
die Tür aufmachen/zumachen, die Tür öffnen/schließen **to open/
  close the door**
das Zimmer betreten **to go into the room**
putzen **to clean**; abstauben **to dust**; staubsaugen **to hoover**
bürsten **to brush**; waschen **to wash**; bügeln **to iron**

USEFUL WORDS *(feminine)*

die Brücke, -n	(narrow) rug
die Daunendecke, -n	eiderdown
die Fußmatte, -n	doormat
die Heizdecke, -n	electric blanket
die Kaffeemühle, -n	coffee grinder
die Leiter, -n	ladder
die Matte, -n	mat
die Nackenrolle, -n	bolster
die Rasierklinge, -n	razor blade
die Röhre, -n	pipe
die Rührmaschine, -n	(electric) mixer
die Satellitenantenne, -n	satellite dish
die Steppdecke, -n	(continental) quilt
die Tapete, -n	wallpaper
die Vase, -n	vase
die Waage, -n	(set of) scales
die Wäscheschleuder, -n	spin dryer

USEFUL WORDS *(neuter)*

das Abwaschtuch, ⸚er	dish cloth
das Bügelbrett, -er	ironing board *or* table
das Bügeleisen	iron
das Dampfbügeleisen	steam iron
das Gemälde	painting, picture
das Geschirrtuch, ⸚er	dish cloth; tea towel
das Polster	cushion; pillow
das Rohr, -e	pipe
das Seifenpulver	soap powder
das Staubtuch, ⸚er	duster

ESSENTIAL WORDS *(masculine)*

der	**Absender (Abs.)**	sender
der	**Anruf, -e**	telephone call
der	**Bescheid, -e**	information
der	**Brief, -e**	letter
der	**Briefkasten, ∺**	postbox, pillar box
der	**Briefträger**	postman
der	**Cent, -s**	cent
der	**Euro, -s**	euro
der	**Fernsprecher**	telephone
der	**Geldbeutel**	purse
der	**Kugelschreiber; der Kuli, -s**	ballpoint pen, Biro®
der	**Kurs, -e**	rate
der	**Name, -n**	name
der	**Polizist, -en**	policeman
der	**Preis, -e**	price, cost
der	**(Reise)scheck, -s**	(traveller's) cheque
der	**Schalter**	counter
der	**(Telefon)hörer**	(telephone) receiver
der	**Umschlag, ∺e**	envelope
der	**Vorname, -n**	first name, Christian name

USEFUL PHRASES

entschuldigen Sie bitte – wo ist der nächste Briefkasten? **excuse me – where is the nearest postbox?**

kennst du dich hier aus? **do you know this place (well)?**

wo bekomme ich Auskunft? **where can I get some information?**

ist es (nach Bremen) noch weit? **do we have far to go (to Bremen)?**

wie komme ich zum Bahnhof? **how do I get to the station?**

geradeaus **straight on**

die erste Straße links **the first street on the left**

die dritte Straße rechts **the third street on the right**

links/rechts abbiegen **to turn left/right**

2 Kilometer nördlich der Stadtmitte **2 kilometres north of the town centre**

ESSENTIAL WORDS *(feminine)*

die	**Adresse, -n** *or* die **Anschrift, -en**	address
die	**Ansichtskarte, -n**	picture postcard
die	**Auskunft, ̈e**	information; directory enquiries
die	**Bank, -en**	bank
die	**Bezahlung, -en**	payment
die	**Briefkarte, -n**	letter card
die	**Briefmarke, -n**	(postage) stamp
die	**Einladung, -en**	invitation
die	**E-Mail, -s**	e-mail
die	**(Hand)tasche, -n**	(hand)bag
die	**Kasse, -n**	cash desk; check-out; till
die	**Münze, -n**	coin
die	**Polizei**	police
die	**Polizeiwache, -n**	police station
die	**Polizistin**	policewoman
die	**Post**	post, mail
die	**Postkarte, -n**	postcard
die	**Reparatur, -en**	repair, repairing
die	**Rückgabe, -n**	return
die	**SIM-Karte, -n**	SIM card
die	**SMS**	text message
die	**Sparkasse, -n**	savings bank
die	**Taste, -n**	(push-)button
die	**Telefonzelle, -n**	callbox, telephone box
die	**Unterschrift, -en**	signature
die	**Vorwahlnummer, -n**	dialling code
die	**Wechselstube, -n**	bureau de change

USEFUL PHRASES

ich habe meine Tasche verloren – hat jemand sie gefunden? **I've lost my bag – has anyone found it?**

beschreiben **to describe**

liegen lassen **to leave behind**; klauen **to pinch**

ein Formular ausfüllen **to fill in a form**

der Bank *(dat)* Bescheid sagen **to inform the bank**

ESSENTIAL WORDS (neuter)

das	**Briefpapier, -e**	writing paper
das	**Fax(gerät), -e**	fax
das	**Formular, -e**	form
das	**Fundbüro, -s**	lost property office
das	**Handy, -s**	mobile phone
das	**Kleingeld**	small change
das	**Mobiltelefon, -e**	mobile phone
das	**Päckchen**	package, (*small*) parcel
das	**Paket, -e**	parcel, package
das	**Portemonnaie, -s**	purse
das	**Postamt, ¨er**	post office
das	**Postwertzeichen**	postage stamp
das	**Problem, -e**	problem
das	**Scheckheft, -e**	cheque book
das	**Telefon, -e**	telephone
das	**Telefonbuch, ¨er**	telephone directory
das	**Verkehrsamt, ¨er**	tourist information office

USEFUL PHRASES

einen Brief schreiben **to write a letter**
aufgeben **to send, post**; senden, schicken **to send**
zur Post gehen **to go to the post office**
den Brief einwerfen **to post the letter (in postbox)**
ein Paket aufgeben **to hand in a parcel**
faxen **to fax**
einige Briefmarken kaufen **to buy some stamps**
was ist das Porto für einen Brief nach Schottland? **how much is a letter to Scotland?**
3 Briefmarken zu 80 Cent **3 80-cent stamps**
ist Post für mich da? **is there any mail for me?**
erwarten **to expect**
bekommen, erhalten **to get, receive**
zurückschicken **to send back**
mit Luftpost **by airmail**
portofrei **freepost**; postlagernd **poste restante**

IMPORTANT WORDS *(masculine)*

der	**Anschluss, ⁻e**	(telephone) extension
der	**Fehler**	fault; mistake, error
der	**ISDN-Anschluss, ⁻e**	ISDN connection
der	**Luftpostbrief, -e**	airmail letter
der	**Personalausweis, -e**	identity card
der	**Postbeamte, -n**	counter clerk
der	**Zeuge, -n**	witness

IMPORTANT WORDS *(feminine)*

die	**(Bank)note, -n**	(bank)note
die	**Beschreibung, -en**	description
die	**Brieftasche, -n**	wallet
die	**Faxnummer, -n**	fax number
die	**Geldstrafe, -n**	fine
die	**Heimat, -en**	home (town/country *etc*)
die	**Leerung, -en**	collection (*of mail*)
die	**Luftpost**	airmail
die	**Nummer, -n**	number
die	**Postbeamtin**	counter clerk
die	**Postgebühr, -en**	postage
die	**Prepaidkarte, -n**	prepaid card
die	**Scheckkarte, -n**	cheque card
die	**Telefonnummer, -n**	phone number
die	**Verabredung, -en**	date, appointment
die	**Verbindung, -en**	line, connection
die	**Währung, -en**	currency

USEFUL PHRASES

ich möchte einen Scheck einlösen **I'd like to cash a cheque**
unterschreiben **to sign**
ich möchte Pfunde (in Euro) umtauschen **I'd like to change some pounds**
(**into euros**)
können Sie mir ein Euro wechseln? **can you give me change of a euro?**
wie viel Geld willst du wechseln? **how much money do you want to change?**
ich habe kein Kleingeld **I don't have any (small) change**
bar bezahlen **to pay in cash**
ein Scheck über 100 Pfund **a cheque for £100**

IMPORTANT WORDS *(neuter)*

das	Bargeld	cash
das	Ferngespräch, -e	trunk call
das	Geschlecht, -er	sex
das	Missverständnis, -se	misunderstanding
das	Ortsgespräch, -e	local call
das	Pfund Sterling	pound sterling
das	R-Gespräch, -e	reverse-charge call
das	Telefongespräch, -e	phone call
das	Telegramm, -e	telegram, cable
das	Termin, -e	*(doctor's etc)* appointment

USEFUL PHRASES

jdn anrufen, mit jdm telefonieren to phone *or* call sb
den Hörer abheben to lift the receiver
ein R-Gespräch führen to make a reverse-charge call
die Nummer suchen/wählen to look up/dial the number
können Sie mir die Vorwahlnummer sagen? can you tell me the dialling code?
drücken to press
das Telefon läutet the phone rings
wer ist am Apparat? who's speaking?
hallo, hier ist ... hello, this is ...
kann ich Peter sprechen? could I speak to Peter?
bleiben Sie am Apparat hold on, please
eine Nachricht hinterlassen to leave a message
besetzt engaged; außer Betrieb out of order
Sie sind falsch verbunden you have the wrong number
ich habe mich verwählt I dialled the wrong number
danke für den Anruf thank you for calling
ich rufe Sie zurück I'll call you back
die Verbindung ist sehr schlecht it's a bad line
den Hörer auflegen *or* einhängen to replace the receiver
mailen to e-mail; simsen to text
eine SMS-Nachricht schicken to send a text message

USEFUL WORDS (masculine)

der	Einschreibebrief, -e	registered letter
der	Empfänger	addressee
der	Stempel	postmark

USEFUL WORDS (feminine)

die	Blockschrift	block capitals (pl)
die	Drucksache, -n	printed matter
die	Kaution, -en	deposit
die	Postanweisung, -en	postal order
die	Postleitzahl, -en	postcode
die	Steuer, -n	tax

USEFUL WORDS (neuter)

das	Branchenverzeichnis, -se	Yellow Pages® (pl)
das	Einschreiben	registered letter
das	Einwickelpapier	wrapping paper
das	Konto, Konten	account
das	Packpapier	brown paper, wrapping paper
das	Porto	postage

USEFUL PHRASES

sprechen Sie Englisch? **do you speak English?**
was heißt das auf Deutsch? **what's that in German?**
könnten Sie das bitte wiederholen? **could you repeat that please?**
verstehen, kapieren **to understand**
wie schreibt man das? **how do you spell that?**
soll ich das buchstabieren? **shall I spell that for you?**
Lieber Franz **Dear Franz**; Liebe Bettina **Dear Bettina**
Sehr geehrter Herr Müller **Dear Mr Müller**; Sehr geehrte Frau Brown
  Dear Mrs Brown
Sehr geehrte Damen und Herren **Dear Sir** or **Madam**
Mit freundlichen Grüßen **Yours sincerely**
Viele Grüße **Love, Best wishes**
Hochachtungsvoll **Yours faithfully**

ESSENTIAL WORDS (masculine)

der	Ausweis, -e	identity card
der	Polizist, -en	policeman
der	Reisescheck, -s	traveller's cheque
der	Scheck, -s	cheque
der	Terrorismus	terrorism

ESSENTIAL WORDS (feminine)

die	Auskunft, ⁻e	information; particulars (pl)
die	Ausweiskarte, -n	identity card
die	Bank, -en	bank
die	Polizei	police
die	Polizistin	policewoman
die	Tasche, -n	bag

ESSENTIAL WORDS (neuter)

das	Fundbüro, -s	lost property office
das	Geld, -er	money
das	Portemonnaie, -s	purse

USEFUL PHRASES

verunglücken to have an accident
jdn überfahren to run sb over
verletzt injured; verwundet wounded
betrunken drunk
Notruf (110) emergency phone number
versichert sein to be insured
Hilfe! help!; haltet den Dieb! stop thief!
Feuer! fire!; Hände hoch! hands up!
Angst haben to be afraid
stehlen to steal; klauen to pinch; rauben to rob
eine Bank überfallen to rob a bank
entführen to kidnap; to hijack
verschwinden to disappear
die Polizei rufen to send for the police
retten to rescue; entkommen to escape; strafen to punish

IMPORTANT WORDS *(masculine)*

der	Bandit, -en	bandit
der	Demonstrant, -en	demonstrator
der	Detektiv, -e	detective
der	Dieb, -e	thief
der	Diebstahl, ¨e	theft
der	Entführer	kidnapper; hijacker
der	Gangster, -s	gangster
die	Geschworenen *(pl)*	jury
der	Privatdetektiv, -e	private detective
der	Retter	rescuer
der	Revolver	gun, revolver
der	Rowdy, -s	hooligan
der	Sicherheitsbeamte, -n	security guard
der	Streit, -e	argument, dispute
der	Taschendieb, -e	pickpocket
der	Terrorist, -en	terrorist
	Tote(r), -n	dead man/woman
der	Überfall, ¨e	raid; attack
der	Unfall, ¨e	accident
der	Zeuge, -n	witness

IMPORTANT WORDS *(neuter)*

das	Bargeld	cash, ready money
das	Gefängnis, -se	prison
das	Gericht, -e	court
das	Gesetz, -e	law
das	Recht, -e	right

USEFUL PHRASES

demonstrieren to demonstrate
ein Gebäude (in die Luft) sprengen to blow up a building
erschießen to shoot (dead)
töten to kill; ermorden to murder
verhaften to arrest; ins Gefängnis kommen to go to jail
schuldig guilty; unschuldig innocent

IMPORTANT WORDS *(feminine)*

die	Armee, -n	army
die	Atomwaffe, -n	atomic weapon
die	Bande, -n	band, gang
die	Beschreibung, -en	description
die	Bombe, -n	bomb
die	Brieftasche, -n	wallet
die	Demonstrantin	demonstrator
die	Demonstration, -en	demonstration
die	Diebin	thief
die	Droge, -n	drug
die	Erlaubnis, -se	permission; permit
die	Gefahr, -en	danger, risk
die	Geldstrafe, -n	fine
die	Notdienste *(pl)*	emergency services
die	Pflicht, -en	duty
die	Pistole, -n	gun, pistol
die	Rettung, -en	rescue
die	Terroristin	terrorist
die	Todesstrafe, -n	death penalty
die	Untersuchung, -en	inquiry, investigation
die	Zeugin	witness

USEFUL WORDS *(neuter)*

das	Gewehr, -e	gun, rifle
das	Heer, -e	army
das	Rauschgift, -e	drug
das	(Todes)urteil, -e	(death) sentence
das	Verbrechen	crime
das	Zuchthaus, -häuser	(top-security) prison

USEFUL WORDS (masculine)

der	Beweis, -e	evidence, proof
der	Brand, ⸚e	fire
der	Einbrecher	burglar
der	Einbruch, ⸚e	burglary, break-in
der	Feind, -e	enemy
	Gefangene(r), -n	prisoner
der	Gefängniswärter	prison guard
der	Gerichtshof, ⸚e	law court
der	Identitätsdiebstahl, ⸚e	identity theft
der	Mord, -e	murder
der	Mörder	murderer, killer
der	Prozess, -e	trial, lawsuit
der	Raub	robbery
der	Räuber	robber
der	Raubüberfall, ⸚e	robbery with violence
der	(Rechts)anwalt, ⸚e	lawyer, barrister
der	Spion, -e	spy
der	Verbrecher	criminal
	Verdächtige(r), -n	suspect

USEFUL WORDS (feminine)

die	Alarmanlage, -n	burglar alarm
die	Belohnung, -en	reward
die	Fahrerflucht	hit-and-run driving
die	Festnahme, -n	arrest
die	Flucht, -en	escape
die	Haft	custody
die	Handschellen (pl)	handcuffs
die	Justiz	justice
die	Leiche, -n	corpse, body
die	(Polizei)wache, -n	police station
die	Regierung, -en	government
die	Schuld	guilt; fault
die	Unschuld	innocence
die	Verhaftung, -en	arrest
die	Versicherungspolice, -n	insurance policy

ESSENTIAL WORDS (*masculine*)

der	**Kaugummi**	chewing gum
der	**Stein, -e**	stone, rock

ESSENTIAL WORDS (*neuter*)

das	**Aluminium**	aluminium
das	**Benzin**	petrol
das	**Dieselöl**	diesel oil
das	**Gas**	gas
das	**Glas**	glass
das	**Gummiband, ̈-er**	rubber band; elastic
das	**Leder**	leather
das	**Öl, -e**	oil
das	**Papier, -e**	paper

USEFUL PHRASES

eine Baumwollbluse a cotton blouse
ein Seidenschal (*m*) a silk scarf
ein Holzstuhl (*m*) a wooden chair
ein Strohhut (*m*) a straw hat
ein Pelzmantel (*m*) a fur coat
ein Wollpullover (*m*) a woollen jumper
ein Pappkarton (*m*) a cardboard box
ein Lammfellmantel (*m*) a sheepskin coat
eine Tasche aus Leder a leather bag
die Tasche ist aus Leder the bag is made of leather
eine Vase aus Ton an earthenware vase
die Vase ist aus Ton the vase is made of earthenware
eisern, Eisen- iron
golden, Gold- gold, golden
hölzern, Holz- wooden
marmorn, Marmor- marble
silbern, Silber- silver
echt real, genuine
kostbar precious; teuer costly, expensive

IMPORTANT WORDS *(masculine)*

der	**Aufkleber**	sticker, label
der	**Denim**	denim
der	**Fleck, -e**	mark, spot
der	**Gips**	plaster; plaster of Paris
der	**Jeansstoff, -e**	denim
der	**Klebstoff, -e**	glue
der	**Kord**	cord, corduroy
der	**Kunststoff, -e**	synthetic
der	**Polyester**	polyester
der	**Stahl**	steel
der	**Stoff, -e**	cloth, material

IMPORTANT WORDS *(feminine)*

die	**Baumwolle**	cotton
die	**Bronze**	bronze
die	**Gebrauchsanweisung, -en**	directions for use *(pl)*
die	**Seide**	silk

IMPORTANT WORDS *(neuter)*

das	**Blei**	lead
das	**Gold**	gold
das	*or der* **Gummi**	rubber; gum
das	**Holz, ⁛er**	wood
das	**Material, -ien**	material(s)
das	**Metall, -e**	metal
das	**Nylon**	nylon
das	**Petroleum**	paraffin
das	**Plastik**	plastic
das	**Seidenpapier**	tissue paper
das	**Silber**	silver
das	**Silberpapier**	silver paper
das	**Stroh**	straw
das	**Vinyl**	vinyl
das	**Wildleder**	suede

USEFUL WORDS *(masculine)*

der	**Backstein, -e**	brick
der	**Beton**	concrete
der	**Bindfaden, ⸚**	string
der	**Draht, ⸚e**	wire
der	**Faden, ⸚**	thread
der	**Kalk**	lime
der	**Karton, -s**	cardboard; cardboard box
der	**Kautschuk**	rubber *(substance)*
der	**Kleb(e)streifen**	adhesive tape
der	**Marmor**	marble
der	**Pelz, -e**	fur
der	**Samt**	velvet
der	**Satin**	satin
der	**Schaumgummi**	foam rubber
der	**Tesafilm**®	Sellotape®
der	**Ton**	clay
der	**Tweed**	tweed
der	**Zement**	cement
der	**Ziegelstein, -e** *or* der **Ziegel**	brick
der	**Zustand, ⸚e**	condition

USEFUL PHRASES

in gutem/schlechtem Zustand **in good/bad condition**
„trocken aufbewahren *or* lagern" **"keep dry"**
etw chemisch reinigen **to dry-clean sth**

USEFUL WORDS *(feminine)*

die	**Flüssigkeit, -en**	liquid
die	**Kohle**	coal
die	**Leinwand**	canvas
die	**Pappe, -n**	cardboard
die	**Plastikfolie, -n**	clingfilm
die	**Schnur, ̈e**	cord, string
die	**Spitze, -n**	lace
die	**Strickwaren** *(pl)*	knitwear
die	**Watte**	cotton wool
die	**Wolle**	wool

USEFUL WORDS *(neuter)*

das	**Acryl**	acrylic
das	**Blech**	tin
das	**Eisen**	iron
das	**Fell, -e**	fur, coat
das	**Kristall**	crystal
das	**Kupfer**	copper
das	**Leinen**	linen
das	**Messing**	brass
das	**Porzellan**	porcelain, china
das	**Schaffell**	sheepskin
das	**Segeltuch**	sailcloth, canvas
das	**Seil, -e**	rope; cable
das	**Stanniolpapier**	tinfoil
das	**Steingut**	earthenware
das	**Styropor**	polystyrene
das	**Wachs**	wax
das	**Zinn**	pewter; tin

ESSENTIAL + IMPORTANT WORDS *(masculine)*

der **Jazz**	jazz
der **Musiker**	musician
der **Triangel**	triangle
der **Zuhörer**	listener; *(pl)* audience

ESSENTIAL + IMPORTANT WORDS *(feminine)*

die **Blaskapelle, -n**	brass band
die **Blockflöte, -n**	recorder
die **Flöte, -n**	flute
die **Geige, -n**	violin, fiddle
die **Gitarre, -n**	guitar
die **Gruppe, -n**	group
die **Kapelle, -n**	band, orchestra
die **Klarinette, -n**	clarinet
die **Musik**	music
die **Note, -n**	note; *(pl)* music
die **Oboe, -n**	oboe
die **Taste, -n**	(piano) key
die **Trompete, -n**	trumpet

IMPORTANT WORDS *(neuter)*

das **Akkordeon, -s**	accordion
das **Bügelhorn, ¨er**	bugle
das **Cello, -s** *or* **Celli**	cello
das **Horn, ¨er**	horn
das **Klavier, -e**	piano
das **Konzert, -e**	concert; concerto
das **(Musik)instrument, -e**	(musical) instrument
das **Orchester**	orchestra; band
das **Saxophon, -e**	saxophone
das **Schlagzeug, -e**	drums *(pl)*
das **Xylophon, -e**	xylophone

USEFUL PHRASES

Klavier/Gitarre spielen to play the piano/the guitar
die Schlagermusik pop music; die klassische Musik classical music;
   die Blasmusik brass band music

USEFUL WORDS *(masculine)*

der Akkord, -e	chord
der Chor, ̈-e	choir; chorus
der Dirigent, -en	conductor
der Dudelsack, ̈-e	bagpipes *(pl)*
der Flügel	grand piano
der Kontrabass, -bässe	double bass
der Solist, -en	soloist
der Taktstock, -stöcke	(conductor's) baton
der Ton, ̈-e	note

USEFUL WORDS *(feminine)*

die Harfe, -n	harp
die Konzerthalle, -n	concert hall
die Mundharmonika, -s *or* -ken	mouth organ, harmonica
die Musikkapelle, -n	band *(circus, military etc)*
die Oper, -n	opera; opera house
die Orgel, -n	organ
die Posaune, -n	trombone
die Querflöte, -n	flute
die Saite, -n	string
die Solistin	soloist
die Tastatur, -en	keyboard
die Tonart, -en	(musical) key
die (große) Trommel, (-n) -n	(big, bass) drum
die Violine, -n	violin
die Ziehharmonika, -s	concertina; accordion

USEFUL WORDS *(neuter)*

das Becken	cymbals *(pl)*
das Fagott, -s *or* -e	bassoon
das Jagdhorn, ̈-er	bugle; hunting horn
das Opernhaus, -häuser	opera house
das Streichorchester	string orchestra
das Tamburin, -e	tambourine
das Violoncello, -s *or* -celli	violoncello
das Waldhorn, ̈-er	French horn

CARDINAL NUMBERS

nought	0	null
one	1	eins
two	2	zwei
three	3	drei
four	4	vier
five	5	fünf
six	6	sechs
seven	7	sieben
eight	8	acht
nine	9	neun
ten	10	zehn
eleven	11	elf
twelve	12	zwölf
thirteen	13	dreizehn
fourteen	14	vierzehn
fifteen	15	fünfzehn
sixteen	16	sechzehn
seventeen	17	siebzehn
eighteen	18	achtzehn
nineteen	19	neunzehn
twenty	20	zwanzig
twenty-one	21	einundzwanzig
twenty-two	22	zweiundzwanzig
twenty-three	23	dreiundzwanzig
thirty	30	dreißig
thirty-one	31	einunddreißig
thirty-two	32	zweiunddreißig
forty	40	vierzig
fifty	50	fünfzig
sixty	60	sechzig
seventy	70	siebzig
eighty	80	achtzig
ninety	90	neunzig
ninety-nine	99	neunundneunzig
a (or one) hundred	100	hundert

CARDINAL NUMBERS (*continued*)

a hundred and one	101	hunderteins
a hundred and two	102	hundertzwei
a hundred and ten	110	hundertzehn
a hundred and eighty-two	182	hundertzweiundachtzig
two hundred	200	zweihundert
two hundred and one	201	zweihunderteins
two hundred and two	202	zweihundertzwei
three hundred	300	dreihundert
four hundred	400	vierhundert
five hundred	500	fünfhundert
six hundred	600	sechshundert
seven hundred	700	siebenhundert
eight hundred	800	achthundert
nine hundred	900	neunhundert
a (*or* one) thousand	1000	(ein)tausend
a thousand and one	1001	tausendundeins
a thousand and two	1002	tausendundzwei
two thousand	2000	zweitausend
ten thousand	10 000	zehntausend
a (*or* one) hundred thousand	100 000	hunderttausend
a (*or* one) million	1 000 000	eine Million
two million	2 000 000	zwei Millionen

USEFUL PHRASES

1979 neunzehnhundertneunundsiebzig
2001 zweitausendundeins

gerade/ungerade Zahlen **even/odd numbers**
50 Prozent **50 per cent**

ORDINAL NUMBERS

These can be masculine, feminine or neuter, and take the appropriate endings.

first	der Erste
second	der Zweite
third	der Dritte
fourth	der Vierte
fifth	der Fünfte
sixth	der Sechste
seventh	der Siebte
eighth	der Achte
ninth	der Neunte
tenth	der Zehnte
eleventh	der Elfte
twelfth	der Zwölfte
thirteenth	der Dreizehnte
fourteenth	der Vierzehnte
fifteenth	der Fünfzehnte
sixteenth	der Sechzehnte
seventeenth	der Siebzehnte
eighteenth	der Achtzehnte
nineteenth	der Neunzehnte
twentieth	der Zwanzigste
twenty-first	der Einundzwanzigste
twenty-second	der Zweiundzwanzigste
thirtieth	der Dreißigste
thirty-first	der Einunddreißigste
fortieth	der Vierzigste
fiftieth	der Fünfzigste
sixtieth	der Sechzigste
seventieth	der Siebzigste
eightieth	der Achtzigste
ninetieth	der Neunzigste
hundredth	der Hundertste
hundred and first	der Hunderterste
hundred and tenth	der Hundertzehnte

ORDINAL NUMBERS *(continued)*

two hundredth	der Zweihundertste
three hundredth	der Dreihundertste
four hundredth	der Vierhundertste
five hundredth	der Fünfhundertste
six hundredth	der Sechshundertste
seven hundredth	der Siebenhundertste
eight hundredth	der Achthundertste
nine hundredth	der Neunhundertste
thousandth	der Tausendste
two thousandth	der Zweitausendste
millionth	der Millionste
two millionth	der Zweimillionste

FRACTIONS

a half	halb, die Hälfte
one and a half kilos	eineinhalb Kilos, anderthalb Kilos
two and a half kilos	zweieinhalb Kilos
a third	ein Drittel *(nt)*
two thirds	zwei Drittel
a quarter	ein Viertel *(nt)*
three quarters	drei Viertel
a sixth	ein Sechstel *(nt)*
five and five sixths	fünf und fünf Sechstel
an eighth	ein Achtel *(nt)*
a twelfth	ein Zwölftel *(nt)*
a twentieth	ein Zwanzigstel *(nt)*
a hundredth	ein Hundertstel *(nt)*
a thousandth	ein Tausendstel *(nt)*
a millionth	ein Millionstel *(nt)*

USEFUL PHRASES

zum x-ten Mal **for the umpteenth time**
ein Millionär **a millionaire**
(0, 4) null Komma vier **(0.4) nought point four**
die Flasche war drei viertel leer **the bottle was three-quarters empty**

NUMBERS AND QUANTITIES

der	Becher (Joghurt)	pot (of yogurt)
ein	bisschen	a little (bit of)
die	Büchse, -n	tin, can
der	*or* das Deziliter	decilitre
das	Dutzend	dozen
	Dutzende von	dozens of
	etwas	a little (bit of)
das	Fass, ̈er	barrel
die	Flasche, -n (Wein)	bottle (of wine)
das	Glas, ̈er (Milch)	glass (of milk)
das	Glas, ̈er Marmelade	jar *or* pot of jam
eine	Halbe	a half (*litre of beer etc*)
ein	halbes Dutzend/ Pfund	half-a-dozen/-pound, a half dozen/pound
ein	halbes Kilo	half a kilo
ein	halber Liter	half a litre
die	Handvoll (Münzen)	handful (of coins)
der	Haufen	heap, pile
ein	Haufen	heaps of
	Hunderte von	hundreds of
	hundert Gramm Käse	a hundred grammes of cheese
die	Kanne, -n (Kaffee)	pot (of coffee)
das	Kilo(gramm)	kilo(gramme)
ein	Kleines	a half pint (*of beer etc*)
das	Knäuel Wolle *or* das Wollknäuel	ball of wool
der	*or* das Liter	litre
die	Menge, -n	crowd; heaps of
der	*or* das Meter (Stoff)	metre (of cloth)
das	Paar (Schuhe)	pair (of shoes)
das	Päckchen	packet
die	Packung Keks/ Zigaretten	packet of biscuits/ cigarettes
das	Pfund (Kartoffeln)	pound (of potatoes)
die	Portion, -en (Eis)	portion *or* helping (of ice cream)

NUMBERS AND QUANTITIES *(continued)*

der	**Riegel Seife**	cake *or* bar of soap
der	**Riegel Schokolade**	bar of chocolate, chocolate bar
die	**Schachtel, -n**	box; packet (*of cigarettes*)
die	**Schar, -en**	group, band
die	**Scheibe, -n (Brot)**	slice (of bread)
die	**Schüssel, -n**	bowl, dish
der	**Stapel**	pile
das	**Stück Zucker**	lump of sugar
das	**Stück Kuchen**	piece *or* slice of cake
das	**Stück Papier**	bit *or* piece of paper
die	**Tafel (-n) Schokolade**	bar of chocolate
die	**Tasse (voll)**	cup(ful)
	Tausende von	thousands of
der	**Teller**	plate
das	**Viertel(pfund)**	quarter(-pound)
ein	**wenig**	a little (bit) of
der	**Würfel Zucker**	lump of sugar
der	**Würfel Margarine**	half a pound of margarine (*in cube shape*)

USEFUL PHRASES

für das Dutzend/das Hundert/das Tausend per dozen/hundred/thousand,
(for) a dozen/a hundred/a thousand

ESSENTIAL WORDS *(masculine)*

der	Artikel	article
der	Ohrring, -e	earring
der	Rasierapparat, -e	razor
der	Ring, -e	ring
der	Schlüsselring, -e	key-ring
der	Schmuck	jewellery

ESSENTIAL WORDS *(feminine)*

die	Armbanduhr, -en	(wrist) watch
die	Haarbürste, -n	hairbrush
die	Halskette, -n	necklace
die	Kette, -n	chain
die	Rasiercreme, -s	shaving cream
die	Sache, -n	thing
die	Schönheit	beauty
die	Seife, -n	soap
die	Zahnbürste, -n	toothbrush
die	Zahnpasta, -pasten	toothpaste

ESSENTIAL + IMPORTANT WORDS *(neuter)*

das	Armband, ̈-er	bracelet
das	Deo, -s	deodorant
das	Gold	gold
das	Haarwaschmittel	shampoo
das	Handtuch, ̈-er	towel
das	Juwel, -en	jewel; *(pl)* jewels, jewellery
das	Make-up	foundation; make-up
das	Parfüm, -s *or* -e	perfume, scent
das	Rasierwasser	after-shave
das	Shampoo, -s	shampoo
das	Silber	silver
das	Taschengeld	pocket money
das	Toilettenwasser	toilet water

USEFUL PHRASES

baden to have a bath; duschen to have a shower
sich die Zähne putzen to brush one's teeth

IMPORTANT WORDS *(masculine)*

der	Ehering, -e	wedding ring
der	Gesichtspuder	face powder
der	Kamm, ¨e	comb
der	Schönheitssalon, -s	beauty salon
der	Spiegel	mirror
der	Tampon, -s	tampon

IMPORTANT WORDS *(feminine)*

die	(Damen)binde	sanitary towel
die	Gesichtscreme, -s	face cream
die	Kosmetik	cosmetics *(pl)*, make-up
die	Perle, -n	pearl; bead
die	Perlenkette, -n	beads, string of beads

USEFUL WORDS *(masculine)*

der	Anhänger	pendant
der	Edelstein, -e	gem, precious stone
der	Lidschatten	eyeshadow
der	Lippenstift, -e	lipstick
der	Lockenwickler	curler, roller
der	Nagellack	nail varnish, nail polish
der	Nagellackentferner	nail varnish remover
der	Trauring, -e	wedding ring
der	Waschbeutel	toilet bag
der	Waschlappen	face flannel

USEFUL WORDS *(feminine)*

die	Brosche, -n	brooch
die	Frisur, -en	hairstyle
die	Krawattennadel, -n	tie-pin
die	Perücke, -n	wig
die	Puderdose, -n	(powder) compact
die	Schminke, -n	make-up
die	Wimperntusche	mascara

USEFUL PHRASES

sich rasieren to shave; kämmen to comb; bürsten to brush

ESSENTIAL WORDS *(masculine)*

der	**Baum, Bäume**	tree
der	**Blumentopf, ¨-e**	flower pot
der	**Garten, ¨-**	garden
der	**Gärtner**	gardener
der	**Gemüsegarten, ¨-**	vegetable garden
der	**Grund**	ground
der	**Obstgarten, ¨-**	orchard
der	**Regen**	rain
der	**Sonnenschein**	sunshine
der	**Stein, -e**	stone, rock

ESSENTIAL WORDS *(feminine)*

die	**Biene, -n**	bee
die	**Blume, -n**	flower
die	**Erde, -n**	earth, soil
die	**(Garten)bank, ¨-e**	(garden) seat *or* bench
die	**Gartentür, -en**	garden gate
die	**Rose, -n**	rose
die	**Sonne**	sun
die	**Wespe, -n**	wasp

ESSENTIAL WORDS *(neuter)*

das	**Blatt, ¨-er**	leaf
das	**Gärtnern**	gardening
das	**Gemüse**	vegetable(s)
das	**Gras**	grass

USEFUL PHRASES

Blumen pflanzen to plant flowers
die Pflanzen wachsen the plants grow
gießen to water
pflücken to pick
ein Strauß Rosen/Veilchen, ein Rosenstrauß/Veilchenstrauß
   a bunch of roses/violets

IMPORTANT WORDS *(masculine)*

der	**Boden, ⸚**	ground, soil
der	**Busch, ⸚e**	bush, shrub
der	**Krokus, - *or* -se**	crocus
der	**Pfad, -e**	path
der	**Rasen**	lawn; turf
der	**Schatten**	shadow; shade
der	**Stamm, ⸚e**	trunk
der	**Steingarten, ⸚**	rockery, rock garden
der	**Weg, -e**	path
der	**Wurm, ⸚er**	worm

IMPORTANT WORDS *(feminine)*

die	**Chrysantheme, -n**	chrysanthemum
die	**Dahlie, -n**	dahlia
die	**Hütte, -n**	hut, shed
die	**Hyazinthe, -n**	hyacinth
die	**Lilie, -n**	lily
die	**Orchidee, -n**	orchid
die	**Pflanze, -n**	plant
die	**Sonnenblume, -n**	sunflower
die	**Tulpe, -n**	tulip

IMPORTANT WORDS *(neuter)*

das	**Gartenhaus, -häuser**	summerhouse
das	**Laub(werk)**	leaves *(pl)*, foliage
das	**Unkraut**	weed(s)
das	**Werkzeug, -e**	tool

USEFUL PHRASES

den Garten umgraben **to dig the garden**
den Rasen mähen **to mow the lawn**
im Schatten eines Baumes **in the shade of a tree**
im Schatten bleiben **to stay in the shade**
allerlei Pflanzen **all kinds of plants**
hier duftet es (gut) **what a nice smell there is here**

USEFUL WORDS *(masculine)*

der **Ast**, ̈e	branch
der **Baumstamm**, ̈e	tree trunk
der **Blumenstrauß**, (-sträuße)	bunch *or* bouquet of flowers
der **Dorn**, -en	thorn
der **Duft**, ̈e	perfume, scent
der **Efeu**	ivy
der **Flieder**	lilac
der **Goldlack**	wallflower
der **Halm**, -e	stalk, blade
der **Löwenzahn**	dandelion
der **Mohn**, -e	poppy
der **Rasenmäher**	lawnmower
der **Rosenstock**, ̈e	rose bush
der **Samen**	seed(s)
der **Schlauch**, Schläuche	garden hose
der **Schmetterling**, -e	butterfly
der **Schubkarren**	wheelbarrow
der **Stachel**, -n	thorn
der **Stängel**; der **Stiel**, -e	stalk, stem
der **Strauch**, Sträucher	shrub
der **Strauß**, Sträuße	bunch *or* bouquet (of flowers)
der **Tau**	dew
der **Weiher**	pond
der **Wintergarten**, ̈	conservatory
der **Zaun**, Zäune	fence
der **Zweig**, -e	branch

USEFUL PHRASES

Unkraut jäten **to do the weeding**
die Hecke schneiden **to cut the hedge**
die Blätter zusammenharken **to rake up the leaves**
umzäunt **fenced in**
sonnig **sunny**; schattig **shady**

USEFUL WORDS *(feminine)*

die	Beere, -n	berry
die	Blüte, -n	blossom
die	Butterblume, -n	buttercup
die	Gartenwicke, -n	sweet pea
die	Gießkanne, -n	watering can
die	Hacke, -n	hoe
die	Harke, -n	rake
die	Hecke, -n	hedge
die	Heckenschere, -n	hedge-cutters, garden shears
die	Hortensie, -n	hydrangea
die	Knospe, -n	bud
die	Leiter, -n	ladder
die	Margerite, -n	daisy
die	Narzisse, -n	narcissus, daffodil
die	Nelke, -n	carnation
die	Osterglocke, -n	daffodil
die	Pforte, -n	(garden) gate
die	Primel, -n	primrose
die	Rabatte, -n	border, flower bed
die	Walze, -n	roller
die	Wurzel, -n	root

USEFUL WORDS *(neuter)*

das	Blumenbeet, -e	flowerbed
das	Gänseblümchen	daisy
das	Geißblatt	honeysuckle
das	Gewächshaus, -häuser	greenhouse
das	Maiglöckchen	lily of the valley
das	Schneeglöckchen	snowdrop
das	Stiefmütterchen	pansy
das	Veilchen	violet
das	Vergissmeinnicht, -e	forget-me-not

ESSENTIAL WORDS *(masculine)*

der	Ausflug, ⸚e	trip, outing
der	Badeanzug, ⸚e	swimming *or* bathing costume
der	Bikini, -s	bikini
der	Dampfer	steamer
der	Fahrgast, ⸚e	passenger
der	Fisch, -e	fish
der	Fischer	fisherman
der	Hafen, ⸚	port, harbour
der	Passagier, -e	passenger
der	Schwimmer	swimmer
der	Seehafen, ⸚	seaport
der	Seemann, (-leute)	sailor, seaman
der	Sonnenschein	sunshine
der	Spaziergang, ⸚e	walk
der	Stein, -e	stone
der	Strand, ⸚e	shore, beach
der	Urlauber	holiday-maker

ESSENTIAL WORDS *(feminine)*

die	Ansichtskarte, -n	postcard
die	Badehose, -n	swimming *or* bathing trunks
die	Fähre, -n	ferry
die	Hafenstadt, ⸚e	port
die	Insel, -n	island
die	Mannschaft, -en	crew
die	Schwimmerin	swimmer
die	See, -n	sea
die	Seekrankheit	seasickness
die	Seeluft	sea air
die	Sonne	sun
die	Sonnenbrille, -n	(pair of) sunglasses
die	Sonnencreme, -s	sun(tan) cream
die	Überfahrt, -en	crossing
die	Urlauberin	holiday-maker

ESSENTIAL WORDS *(neuter)*

das	Ausland	abroad
das	Bad, ̈-er	bathe (*in sea*), swim
das	Badetuch, ̈-er	(bath) towel
das	Boot, -e	boat
das	Fischerboot, -e	fishing boat
das	Meer, -e	ocean, sea
das	Picknick, -e *or* -s	picnic
das	Ruder	oar; rudder
das	Schiff, -e	ship, vessel
das	Schwimmen	swimming
das	Sonnenöl, -e	suntan oil
das	Wasser	water

IMPORTANT WORDS *(masculine)*

der	Anker	anchor
	Badende(r), -n	bather, swimmer
der	Bord, -e	board
der	Horizont	horizon
der	(Meeres)boden	bottom (of the sea)
der	Ozean, -e	ocean
der	Prospekt, -e	leaflet, brochure
der	Rettungsring, -e	lifebelt
der	Sand, -e	send
der	Segler	sailor, yachtsman
der	Sonnenbrand, ̈-e	sunburn

USEFUL PHRASES

zwei Wochen Urlaub **two weeks' holiday**
am Meer **at the seaside**
ans Meer *or* an die See fahren **to go to the seaside**
es ist Flut/Ebbe **the tide is in/out**
schwimmen gehen **to go for a swim;** sich ausruhen **to have a rest**
sich sonnen **to sunbathe;** am Strand **on the beach**
eine Sonnenbrille tragen **to wear sunglasses**
braun werden **to get a tan**
einen Sonnenbrand bekommen **to get sunburnt**

IMPORTANT WORDS (feminine)

die **Flagge**, -n	flag
die **Küste**, -n	coast, shore; seaside
die **Luftmatratze**, -n	lilo®, airbed
die **Seglerin**	sailor, yachtswoman
die **Vergnügungsfahrt**, -en	pleasure cruise

IMPORTANT WORDS (neuter)

das **Reisebüro**, -s	travel agent's
das **Segel**	sail
das **Segeln**	sailing
das **Teleskop**, -e	telescope
das **Ufer**	shore (*lake*); bank (*river*)

USEFUL WORDS (masculine)

der **Eimer**	bucket
der **Jachthafen**, ¨	marina
der **Kahn**, ¨e	(*small*) boat
der **Kai**, -e *or* -s	quay, quayside
der **Kieselstein**, -e	pebble
der **Krebs**, -e	crab
der **Leuchtturm**, ¨e	lighthouse
der **Liegestuhl**, ¨e	deckchair
der **Mast**, -e(n)	mast
der **Matrose**, -n	sailor
der **Pier**, -e *or* -s	pier
der **Rettungsschwimmer**	lifeguard
der **Schaum**	foam
der **Schiffbruch**, ¨e	shipwreck
der **Schornstein**, ¨e	funnel
der **(See)tang**, -e	seaweed
der **Sonnenstich**, -e	sunstroke
der **Spaten**	spade

USEFUL WORDS *(feminine)*

die	**Boje, -n**	buoy
die	**Bucht, -en**	bay
die	**Ebbe, -n**	low tide
die	**Fahne, -n**	flag
die	**Flotte, -n**	navy, fleet
die	**Flut, -en**	high tide
die	**Jacht, -en**	yacht
die	**Klippe, -n**	cliff
die	**Kreuzfahrt, -en**	cruise
die	**Last, -en**	load, cargo
die	**Möwe, -n**	seagull
die	**Muschel(schale), -n (-n)**	shell
die	**Pauschalreise, -n**	package tour
die	**Sandburg, -en**	sandcastle
die	**(Schiffs)ladung, -en**	cargo
die	**Schwimmweste, -n**	life jacket
die	**(Sonnen)bräune**	(sun)tan
die	**Strömung, -en**	current
die	**Welle, -n**	wave

USEFUL WORDS *(neuter)*

das	**Deck, -s or -e**	deck (*of ship*)
das	**Fahrgeld, -er**	fare
das	**Floß, ̈e**	raft
das	**Steuer**	helm, tiller
das	**Surfbrett, -er**	surfboard
das	**Tretboot, -e**	pedal-boat, pedalo

USEFUL PHRASES

eine Bootsfahrt machen **to go on a boat trip**
an Bord gehen **to go on board**
ruhig **calm**; stürmisch **stormy**; bewegt **choppy**
seekrank werden **to get seasick**
untergehen **to go under**
ertrinken **to drown**

ESSENTIAL WORDS (masculine)

der **Artikel**	article
der **Bäcker**	baker
der **Cent, -s**	cent
der **Einkauf, -käufe**	shopping; purchase
der **Euro, -s**	euro
der **Fahrstuhl, ⸚e**	lift
der **Franken**	(Swiss) franc
der **Geldbeutel**	purse
der **Geschäftsmann, -leute**	businessman
der **Groschen**	10-pfennig piece; groschen
der **Kiosk, -e**	kiosk
der **Kunde, -n**	customer, client
der **Laden, ⸚**	shop
der **Markt, ⸚e**	market
der **Preis, -e**	price
der **Rappen**	centime
der **Schalter**	counter (post office, bank etc)
der **Scheck, -s**	cheque
der **Schein, -e**	(bank)note
der **Schuhmacher**	shoemaker, shoe repairer
der **Sommerschlussverkauf**	summer sale
der **Supermarkt, ⸚e**	supermarket

USEFUL PHRASES

einkaufen gehen to go shopping
Einkäufe machen to do the shopping
Schlange stehen to queue up
kaufen to buy; verkaufen to sell; jdn bedienen to serve sb
kann ich Ihnen behilflich sein? can I help you?
was darf es sein, bitte? what would you like?
ich möchte ... I'd like...; ich brauche ... I need ...
etw bezahlen to pay for sth
etwas stimmt nicht there's something wrong somewhere
ich möchte mich nur mal umsehen I'm just looking

ESSENTIAL WORDS *(feminine)*

die	**Apotheke, -n**	chemist's, pharmacy
die	**Bäckerei, -en**	bakery, baker's (shop)
die	**Bank, -en**	bank
die	**Bibliothek, -en**	library
die	**Buchhandlung, -en**	bookshop, bookseller's
die	**Drogerie, -n**	(retail) chemist's
die	**Etage, -n**	floor
die	**Farbe, -n**	colour
die	**Geschäftszeit, -en**	business hours
die	**Größe, -n**	size
die	**Handlung, -en**	shop
die	**Kasse, -n**	till; cash desk, checkout
die	**Konditorei, -en**	cake shop
die	**Kreditkarte, -n**	credit card
die	**Kundin**	customer, client
die	**Liste, -n**	list
die	**Metzgerei, -en**	butcher's (shop)
die	**Öffnungszeit, -en**	opening time
die	**Post, Postämter**	post office
die	**Rechnung, -en**	bill
die	**Schachtel, -n**	box
die	**Schuhgröße, -n**	shoe size
die	**Selbstbedienung (SB)**	self-service
die	**Sparkasse, -n**	savings bank
die	**Tierhandlung, -en**	pet shop
die	**Tüte, -n**	bag

USEFUL PHRASES

erhältlich **available**; ausverkauft **sold out**
beim Bäcker/Fleischer **at the baker's/butcher's**
anbieten **to offer**; etw probieren **to try sth (taste, sample)**
etw anprobieren **to try sth on**
das gefällt mir **I like that**
wählen **to choose**; wiegen **to weigh**

ESSENTIAL WORDS (neuter)

das	Andenken	souvenir
das	Büro, -s	office
das	Café, -s	café
das	Einkaufen	shopping
das	Erdgeschoss, -e	ground level, ground floor
das	Geld	money
das	Geschäft, -e	shop; trade, business; deal
das	Geschenk, -e	present, gift
das	Kaufhaus, -häuser	department store
das	Kleingeld	small change
das	Portemonnaie, -s	purse
das	Postamt, -̈er	post office
das	Restaurant, -s	restaurant
das	Schuhgeschäft, -e	shoe shop
das	Sonderangebot, -e	bargain (offer), special offer
das	Souvenir, -s	souvenir
das	Warenhaus, -häuser	department store
das	Wirtshaus, -häuser	pub, inn

USEFUL PHRASES

was kostet das? what does it cost?

was macht das? what does that come to?

ich habe 15 Euro dafür bezahlt I paid 15 euros for it

einen Scheck ausstellen to write out a cheque

bar bezahlen to pay cash

Geld für Pralinen ausgeben to spend money on chocolates

zu teuer too dear; ganz billig quite cheap

kostenlos free, free of charge; umsonst for nothing

preiswert good value; ein preiswertes Angebot a bargain

das habe ich günstig bekommen I got it at a good price

das ist aber günstig! what a bargain!

Montags Ruhetag closed on Mondays

IMPORTANT WORDS *(masculine)*

der	Apotheker	(dispensing) chemist
der	Aufzug, ̈e	lift
der	Ausverkauf, -käufe	sale
die	Betriebsferien *(pl)*	holidays *(of a business)*
der	Bioladen, -läden	organic food shop
der	Buchhändler	bookseller
der	Einkaufskorb, -körbe	shopping basket
der	Einkaufswagen	shopping trolley
der	Fischhändler	fishmonger
der	Fleischer	butcher
der	Friseur, -e	hairdresser
der	Händler	dealer
der	Herrenfriseur, -e	barber, men's hairdresser
der	Juwelier	jeweller
der	Kassenzettel	receipt
der	Kaufmann, -leute	merchant
der	Konditor, -en	confectioner
der	Metzger	butcher
der	Obst- und Gemüsehändler	greengrocer
der	Obsthändler	fruiterer
der	Ökoladen, -läden	wholefood shop
der	Schlussverkauf, -käufe	(end-of-season) sale
der	Sonderpreis, -e	special price
der	Tabakladen, ̈	tobacconist's (shop)
der	Umtausch	exchange *(of goods)*
der	Verkauf, -käufe	sale
der	Verkäufer	salesman, shop assistant
der	Waschsalon, -s	laundrette
der	Zeitungshändler	newsagent

USEFUL PHRASES

GmbH Ltd
AG plc

IMPORTANT WORDS (feminine)

die	Abteilung, -en	department
die	Anprobe, -n	trying on
die	Auswahl (an + dat)	choice (of)
die	Brieftasche, -n	wallet
die	Firma, Firmen	firm, company
die	Fleischerei, -en	butcher's (shop)
die	Friseuse, -n	hairdresser
die	Gaststätte, -n	restaurant; pub
die	Kneipe, -n	pub
die	Kundenkarte, -n	charge card
die	Packung, -en	packet, box
die	Parfümerie, -n	perfume counter *or* shop
die	Quittung, -en	receipt
die	Schaufensterpuppe, -n	dummy, model
die	Schlange, -n	queue
die	Schreibwarenhandlung, -en	stationer's
die	Theke, -n	counter (*in café, bar etc*)
die	Verkäuferin	salesgirl, shop assistant
die	Waren (*pl*)	goods, wares

IMPORTANT WORDS (neuter)

das	Einkaufszentrum, -tren	shopping centre
das	Internetcafé, -s	Internet café
das	Juweliergeschäft, -e	jeweller's (shop)
das	Mediencenter	media centre
das	Milchgeschäft, -e	dairy
das	Obergeschoss, -e	upper floor
das	Produkt, -e	product; (*pl*) produce
das	Reisebüro, -s	travel agent's
das	Schaufenster	shop window
das	Untergeschoss, -e	basement

USEFUL PHRASES

einen Schaufensterbummel machen to go window-shopping

USEFUL WORDS (masculine)

der	Buchmacher	bookmaker, "bookie"
der	Einkaufsbummel	shopping spree
der	Eisenwarenhändler	ironmonger
der	(Flick)schuster	cobbler, shoe repairer
der	Gelegenheitskauf, -käufe	bargain
der	Grundstücksmakler	estate agent
der	Gutschein, -e	voucher
der	Handel	trade, business
der	Ladentisch, -e	counter (in shop)
der	Lebensmittelhändler	grocer
der	Optiker	optician
der	Uhrmacher	watchmaker
der	Waschsalon, -s	laundrette

USEFUL WORDS (feminine)

die	Bausparkasse, -n	building society
die	Besorgung, -en	errand; purchase
die	Bücherei, -en	library
die	Bude, -n	stall
die	Eisenwarenhandlung, -en	ironmonger's, hardware shop
die	Filiale, -n	branch
die	Garantie, -n	guarantee
die	Kragenweite, -n	collar size
die	Reinigung, -en	cleaner's
die	Rolltreppe, -n	escalator
die	Versicherungsgesellschaft, -en	insurance company
die	Videothek, -en	video shop
die	Wäscherei, -en	laundry, cleaner's

USEFUL WORDS (neuter)

das	Erzeugnis, -se	product; produce
das	Lebensmittelgeschäft, -e	grocer's, general food store
das	Wechselgeld	change

ESSENTIAL WORDS *(masculine)*

der Ball, ⸚e	ball
der Fußball, ⸚e	football
der Fußballfan, -s	football supporter
der Fußballspieler	footballer
der Läufer	runner
der Pass, ⸚e	pass
der Radsport	cycling
der Rollschuh, -e	roller skate
der Schlittschuh, -e	ice skate
der Spieler	player
der Sport, -e	sport, game
der Sportplatz, ⸚e	sports ground, playing field
der Wintersport	winter sport(s)

ESSENTIAL WORDS *(neuter)*

das Angeln	fishing, angling
das Endspiel, -e	final(s)
das Fitnesszentrum, -tren	health club
das Freibad, ⸚er	open-air swimming pool
das Hallenbad, ⸚er	indoor swimming pool
das Hockey	hockey
das Kricket	cricket
das Laufen	running
das Radfahren	cycling
das Reiten	horse-riding
das Rudern	rowing
das Rugby	rugby
das Schlittschuhlaufen	(ice) skating
das Schwimmbad, ⸚er	swimming baths
das Schwimmen	swimming
das Spiel, -e	play; game, match
das Squash	squash
das Stadion, -ien	stadium
das Tennis	tennis
das Turnen	gymnastics

IMPORTANT WORDS *(masculine)*

der	Basketball, ⁀e	basketball
der	Fußballplatz, ⁀e	football pitch
der	Golfplatz, ⁀e	golf course
der	Golfschläger	golf club *(stick)*
der	Netzball, ⁀e	netball
der	Platz, ⁀e	ground, playing field
der	Pokal, -e	cup
der	Profi, -s	pro
der	Schläger	racket/bat/club *etc*
der	Ski, -er	ski
der	Teilnehmer	participant
der	Tennisplatz, ⁀e	tennis court
der	Volleyball, ⁀e	volleyball
der	Zuschauer	spectator

ESSENTIAL + IMPORTANT WORDS *(feminine)*

die	Angelrute, -n	fishing rod
die	Bundesliga	football league
die	Fußballelf, -en	football team
die	Halbzeit, -en	half *(of match)*; half-time
die	Leichtathletik	athletics
die	Mannschaft, -en	team
die	Rennbahn, -en	racecourse, track
die	Spielerin	player
die	Spielhälfte, -n	half *(of match)*
die	Turnhalle, -n	gym(nasium)
die	Weltmeisterschaft, -en	world championship(s)

USEFUL PHRASES

treibst du gern Sport? **do you like sports?**
spielen **to play**; laufen **to run**; werfen **to throw**;
springen **to jump**; trainieren **to train**; joggen **to go jogging**
üben **to practise**; trimmen **to do exercises**
gewinnen **to win**; verlieren **to lose**
unentschieden enden **to end in a draw**

IMPORTANT WORDS (neuter)

das	**Billard**	billiards
das	**Boxen**	boxing
das	**Ergebnis, -se**	result
das	**Golf(spiel)**	golf
das	**Jogging**	jogging
das	**Netz, -e**	net
das	**Pferderennen**	horse racing; horse-race
das	**Rennen**	racing, race meeting
das	**Schießen**	shooting
das	**Segeln**	sailing
das	**Skateboard, -s**	skateboard
das	**Skifahren; das Skilaufen**	skiing
das	**Snowboard, -s**	snowboard
das	**Tauchen**	(underwater) diving
das	**Tischtennis**	table tennis
das	**Tor, -e**	goal
das	**Ziel, -e**	goal, aim; finish, finishing post

USEFUL WORDS (neuter)

das	**Bergsteigen**	mountaineering
das	**Bogenschießen**	archery
das	**gemischte Doppel**	mixed doubles
das	**Drachenfliegen**	hang-gliding
das	**Fechten**	fencing
das	**Gleitschirmfliegen**	paragliding
das	**Jagen**	hunting; shooting
das	**Klettern**	climbing, mountaineering
die	**Olympischen Spiele** (pl)	Olympic Games
das	**Ringen**	wrestling
das	**Surfbrett**	surfboard
das	**Tauziehen**	tug-of-war
das	**Training**	training
das	**Turnier, -e**	tournament
das	**Wasserski**	water-skiing

USEFUL WORDS *(masculine)*

der	Bergsteiger	mountaineer
der	Federball, ̈e	badminton; shuttlecock
der	Gegner	opponent
der	Hochsprung, ̈e	high jump
der	Kampf, ̈e	fight; contest
der	Meister	champion
der	Rodel	toboggan
der	Satz, ̈e	set *(tennis)*
der	Schiedsrichter	referee; umpire
der	Schlitten	sledge, sleigh
der	Sieger	winner
der	Stoß, ̈e	kick; push, thrust
der	Titelverteidiger	title-holder
der	Torwart, -e	goalkeeper
der	Trainer	trainer, coach; manager
die	Turnschuhe *(pl)*	tennis *or* gym shoes
	Unparteiische(r), -n	umpire; referee
der	Weitsprung, ̈e	long jump
der	(Welt)rekord, -e	(world) record
der	Wettbewerb, -e	competition
der	Wettkampf, ̈e	match, contest

USEFUL WORDS *(feminine)*

die	(Aschen)bahn, -en	(cinder) track
die	Bundesliga	national league
die	Eisbahn, -en	ice rink, skating rink
die	Kegelbahn, -en	bowling alley; skittle alley
die	Meisterschaft, -en	championship
die	Partie, -n	game, match
die	Punktzahl, -en	score
die	Runde, -n	lap, round
die	Siegerin	winner
die	Stoppuhr, -en	stopwatch
die	(Tabellen)spitze, -n	lead *(in league etc)*
die	Tribüne, -n	stand

ESSENTIAL WORDS (masculine)

der	Ausgang, ̈-e	exit, way out
der	Eingang, ̈-e	entrance, way in
der	Film, -e	film
der	Kinobesucher	cinema-goer
der	Quatsch	rubbish
der	Theaterbesucher	theatre-goer
die	Zuhörer (pl)	audience (listeners)

ESSENTIAL WORDS (feminine)

die	Eintrittskarte, -n	ticket
die	Freizeit	free or spare time
die	Handlung, -en	plot, action
die	Kasse, -n	box office, ticket office
die	Musik	music
die	Reservierung, -en	booking
die	(Theater)karte, -n	(theatre) ticket
die	(Theater)kasse, -n	box office
die	Vorstellung, -en	performance, show

ESSENTIAL WORDS (neuter)

das	Kino, -s	cinema
das	Konzert, -e	concert
das	Spiel	acting; play
das	Theater	theatre
das	(Theater)stück, -e	play

USEFUL PHRASES

ich gehe gern ins Kino/ins Theater I like going to the cinema/the theatre
an der Vorverkaufskasse at the booking office
„ausverkauft" "sold out"
mein Lieblingsfilmstar my favourite film star
ein Film mit Untertiteln a film with subtitles
spannend exciting; langweilig boring
(kaum) sehenswert (hardly) worth seeing

IMPORTANT WORDS (masculine)

der	Applaus, -e	applause
der	Balkon, -s or -e	(dress) circle
der	Bühneneingang, -e	stage door
der	Dramatiker	dramatist, playwright
der	(Film)star, -s	(film) star
der	Komiker	comedian
der	Konzertsaal, -säle	concert hall
der	Krieg, -e	war
der	Krimi, -s	thriller
der	Kritiker	critic
der	Rang, -e	circle (in theatre)
der	Saal, Säle	hall; room
der	Schauspieler	actor
der	(Sitz)platz, -e	seat
der	Spaß	fun
der	Spielplan, -e	programme
der	Text, -e	script
der	Titel	title
der	Untertitel	subtitle
der	Videoclip, -s	video clip
der	Vorhang, -e	curtain
der	Western, -s	western
die	Zuschauer (pl)	audience (viewers)
der	erste Rang	dress circle
der	zweite Rang	upper circle

USEFUL PHRASES

die Bühne betreten to step onto the stage
meine Damen und Herren! ladies and gentlemen!
ein Stück geben to put on a play
mit X und Y in den Hauptrollen with X and Y in the main roles
klatschen to clap

IMPORTANT WORDS (feminine)

die	**Aufführung, -en**	performance
die	**Bühne, -n**	stage, platform
die	**Ermäßigung, -en**	reduction
die	**Figur, -en**	character
die	**Garderobe, -n**	cloakroom; wardrobe
die	**Hauptrolle, -n**	main role *or* part
die	**Komödie, -n**	comedy
die	**Oper, -n**	opera; opera house
die	**Reklame, -n**	advertisement
die	**Rolle, -n**	role, part
die	**Saison, -s**	season
die	**Schauspielerin**	actress
die	**Schlange, -n**	queue
die	**Seifenoper, -n**	soap opera
die	**Show, -s**	show
die	**Szene, -n**	scene
die	**Theatergruppe, -n**	dramatic society
die	**Tragödie, -n**	tragedy

IMPORTANT WORDS (neuter)

das	**Ballett, -e**	ballet
das	**Drama, Dramen**	drama
das	**Foyer, -s**	foyer
das	**Kostüm, -e**	costume
das	**Kriminalstück, -e**	thriller
das	**Make-up**	make-up
das	**Musical, -s**	musical
das	**Opernglas, ̈-er**	(pair of) opera glasses
das	**Orchester**	orchestra; band
das	**Parkett, -e**	stalls *(pl)*
das	**Schauspiel, -e**	play
das	**Schauspielhaus, -häuser**	theatre

USEFUL WORDS *(masculine)*

der	Abgang, ⁝e	exit *(of actor)*
der	Auftritt, -e	entrance *(of actor)*; scene *(of play)*
der	Beifall	applause
der	Intendant, -en	stage manager
der	Orchesterraum, -räume	orchestra pit
der	Produzent, -en	(film) producer
der	Regisseur, -e	producer; director
der	Souffleur, -e	prompter
der	Spielfilm, -e	feature film
der	Western	western

USEFUL WORDS *(feminine)*

die	Farce, -n	farce
die	Galerie, -n	the "gods", gallery
die	Generalprobe, -n	dress rehearsal
die	Inszenierung, -en	production
die	Kapelle, -n	band
die	Kritik, -en	review
die	Leinwand, ⁝e	screen
die	Loge, -n	box
die	Pause, -n	interval
die	Platzanweiserin	usherette, attendant
die	Probe, -n	rehearsal
die	Schauspielkunst	acting
die	Souffleuse, -n	prompter
die	Tribüne, -n	platform
die	Zugabe, -n	encore

USEFUL WORDS *(neuter)*

das	Lustspiel, -e	comedy
das	Plakat, -e	poster, notice
das	Rampenlicht	footlights *(pl)*
das	Scheinwerferlicht, -er	spotlight
das	Trauerspiel, -e	tragedy

ESSENTIAL WORDS *(masculine)*

der Abend, -e	evening
der Augenblick, -e	moment, instant
der Beginn, -e	beginning
der Mittag, -e	mid-day, noon
der Moment, -e	moment
der Monat, -e	month
der Morgen	morning
der Nachmittag, -e	afternoon
der Tag, -e	day
der Vormittag, -e	morning
der Wecker	alarm clock

ESSENTIAL WORDS *(feminine)*

die Armbanduhr, -en	(wrist) watch
die Jahreszeit, -en	season
die Minute, -n	minute
die Mitte	middle
die Mitternacht, ¨e	midnight
die Nacht, ¨e	night; night-time
die Sekunde, -n	second
die halbe Stunde, -n -n	half-hour, half-an-hour
die Stunde, -n	hour
die Tageszeit, -en	daytime
die Uhr, -en	clock; time
die Viertelstunde, -n	quarter of an hour
die Weile, -n	while, short time
die Woche, -n	week
die Zeit, -en	time

ESSENTIAL WORDS *(neuter)*

das Datum, Daten	date
das Ende, -n	end
das Jahr, -e	year
das Jahrhundert, -e	century
das Mal, -e	time, occasion
das Wochenende, -n	weekend

USEFUL PHRASES

um 7 Uhr aufstehen **to get up at 7 o'clock**
um 11 Uhr zu Bett gehen **to go to bed at 11 o'clock**
wie viel Uhr ist es?, wie spät ist es? **what time is it?**
den Wievielten haben wir heute? **what is today's date?**
früh **early**; spät **late**; bald **soon**; später **later**
fast **almost**; pünktlich **punctual**
es ist gerade *or* Punkt 2 Uhr **it is exactly 2 o'clock**
halb 3 **half past 2**; halb 9 **half past 8**
gegen 8 Uhr **round about 8 o'clock**
es ist Viertel nach 5/Viertel vor 5 **it is a quarter past 5/a quarter to 5**

vorgestern	the day before yesterday
gestern	yesterday
am vorigen *or* **vorhergehenden Tag**	the day before, the previous day
heute	today
heute Abend	tonight
morgen	tomorrow
am nächsten *or* **folgenden Tag**	the next *or* following day
übermorgen	the day after tomorrow
am übernächsten Tag	two days later
vierzehn Tage	a fortnight

USEFUL PHRASES

morgens **in the morning**; nachmittags **in the afternoon**
abends **in the evening**; nachts **at night, by night**
tagsüber, am Tage **during the day**; stündlich **hourly**
täglich **daily**; wöchentlich **weekly**
monatlich **monthly**; jährlich **annually**; heutzutage **nowadays**

IMPORTANT WORDS *(feminine)*

die **Essenszeit, -en**	mealtime
die **Gelegenheit, -en**	opportunity, occasion
die **Kuckucksuhr, -en**	cuckoo clock
die **Uhrzeit, -en**	time of day

USEFUL PHRASES

einen Augenblick! just a minute!

in diesem/dem Augenblick at this/that moment

im selben Augenblick at that very moment

ich habe keine Zeit (dazu) I have no time (for it)

(sich) die Zeit vertreiben to pass the time

es ist Zeit zum Essen it is time for lunch (dinner etc)

eine Zeit lang bleiben to stay for a while

anderthalb Stunden warten to wait an hour and a half

damals at that time

nie, niemals never; jemals ever

diesmal this time; ein anderes Mal another time

nächstes Mal next time

das erste/letzte Mal the first/last time

zum ersten/letzten Mal for the first/last time

am Wochenende at the weekend

über das Wochenende for the weekend

ich habe es eilig I'm in a hurry

ich habe keine Eile I'm in no hurry

es hat keine Eile there's no hurry

USEFUL WORDS (*masculine*)

der	**Einbruch der Nacht**	nightfall
der	**Kalender**	calendar
der	**Tagesanbruch**	daybreak
der	**(Uhr)zeiger**	hand (*of clock etc*)
der	**Zeitabschnitt, -e**	time, period

USEFUL WORDS (*feminine*)

die	**Epoche, -n**	epoch, period
die	**Gegenwart**	present (*time, tense*)
die	**Mittagszeit, -en**	lunch time
die	**Pause, -n**	interval; pause, break
die	**Standuhr, -en**	grandfather clock
die	**Stoppuhr, -en**	stopwatch
die	**Vergangenheit**	past (*time, tense*)
die	**Verspätung, -en**	delay (*of vehicle*)
die	**Zukunft**	future (*time, tense*)

USEFUL WORDS (*neuter*)

das	**Futur(um)**	future tense
das	**Jahrtausend, -e**	millennium
das	**Jahrzehnt, -e**	decade
das	**Mittelalter**	the Middle Ages
das	**Präsens**	present tense
das	**Schaltjahr, -e**	leap year
das	**Zeitalter**	age, time
das	**Zifferblatt, ̈-er**	(clock) face, dial

USEFUL PHRASES

vor einer Woche/einem Monat/2 Jahren a week/a month/2 years ago
gestern/heute vor einer Woche a week ago yesterday/today
gestern/heute vor 2 Jahren 2 years ago yesterday/today
in einer Woche/einem Monat/2 Jahren in a week('s time)/a month('s time)/
  2 years(' time)
morgen/heute in einer Woche a week tomorrow/today

ESSENTIAL + IMPORTANT WORDS (masculine)

der	Bastler	handyman
der	Bohrer	drill
der	Dosenöffner	tin-opener
der	Hammer, ¨	hammer
der	Holzhammer, ¨	mallet
der	Klebstoff, -e	glue
der	Korkenzieher	corkscrew
der	Schlüssel	key

ESSENTIAL + IMPORTANT WORDS (feminine)

die	Batterie, -n	battery
die	Baustelle, -n	building site
die	Gabel, -n	fork
die	Maschine, -n	machine; engine
die	Werkstatt, ¨en	workshop

ESSENTIAL + IMPORTANT WORDS (neuter)

das	Ding, -e	thing, object
das	Do-it-yourself	do-it-yourself, D.I.Y.
das *or der*	Gummi	rubber; gum
das	Gummiband, ¨er	rubber band; elastic
das	Kabel	wire; cable
das	Schloss, ¨er	lock

USEFUL WORDS (neuter)

das	Brett, -er	plank, board; shelf
das	Gerüst, -e	scaffolding
das	Seil, -e	rope, cable
das	Tau, -e	rope
das	Werkzeug, -e	tool

USEFUL PHRASES

basteln: er kann gut basteln **he is good with his hands**
wozu benutzt man ...? **what do you use ... for?**
reparieren **to repair**; etw reparieren lassen **to have sth repaired**
nageln **to nail**; sägen **to saw**

USEFUL WORDS (masculine)

der	Bolzen	bolt
der	Büchsenöffner	tin-opener
der	Draht, ⁻e	wire
der	Flaschenöffner	bottle-opener
der	Hobel	plane
der	Kleb(e)streifen	adhesive tape
der	Meißel	chisel
der	Nagel, ⁻	nail
der	Pickel	pick, pickaxe
der	Pinsel	paintbrush
der	Pressluftbohrer	pneumatic drill
der	Schraubenschlüssel	spanner
der	Schraubenzieher	screwdriver
der	Schraubstock, ⁻e	vice
der	Stacheldraht, ⁻e	barbed wire
der	Stift, -e	peg
der	Tesafilm®	Sellotape®
der	Werkzeugkasten, ⁻	toolbox

USEFUL WORDS (feminine)

die	Feder, -n	spring, coil
die	Feile, -n	file
die	Heftzwecke, -n	drawing pin, thumbtack
die	Kelle, -n	trowel
die	Leiter, -n	ladder
die	Nadel, -n	needle; pin
die	Planke, -n	plank
die	Reißzwecke, -n	drawing pin, thumbtack
die	Säge, -n	saw
die	Schaufel	shovel; scoop
die	Schere, -n	(pair of) scissors
die	Schnur, ⁻e	string, cord; wire, flex
die	Schraube, -n	screw
die	Wasserwaage, -n	spirit level
die	Zange, -n	(pair of) pliers

ESSENTIAL WORDS (masculine)

der	Bahnhof, ¨e	railway station
der	Bürgersteig, -e	pavement
der	Busbahnhof, ¨e	bus or coach station
der	Dom, -e	cathedral
der	Laden, ¨	shop
der	Markt, ¨e	market
der	Markttag, -e	market day
der	Park, -s	(public) park
der	Parkplatz, ¨e	parking place; car park
der	Polizist, -en	policeman
der	Turm, ¨e	tower
der	Weg, -e	way

ESSENTIAL WORDS (feminine)

die	Brücke, -n	bridge
die	Burg, -en	castle
die	Bushaltestelle, -n	bus stop
die	Ecke, -n	corner, turning
die	Einbahnstraße, -n	one-way street
die	Fabrik, -en	factory, works
die	Fahrt, -en	journey
die	Haltestelle, -n	(bus or tram) stop
die	Hauptstraße, -n	main road; main street
die	Innenstadt, ¨e	city centre, town centre
die	Kirche, -n	church
die	Klinik, -en	hospital, clinic
die	Polizei	police
die	(Polizei)wache, -n	police station
die	Post, Postämter	post office
die	Reise, -n or die Rundfahrt, -en	tour
die	Stadt, ¨e	town; city
die	Straße, -n	street, road
die	Straßenecke, -n	street corner
die	Tankstelle, -n	service station, garage
die	U-Bahn, -en	underground (railway)

ESSENTIAL WORDS *(neuter)*

das	**Büro, -s**	office
das	**Geschäft, -e**	shop
das	**Heft, -e**	book (*of tickets*)
das	**Hotel, -s**	hotel
das	**Kaufhaus, -häuser**	department store
das	**Kino, -s**	cinema
das	**Krankenhaus, -häuser**	hospital
das	**Museum, Museen**	museum
das	**Parken**	parking
das	**Parkhaus, -häuser**	(covered) car park
das	**Postamt, ̈er**	post office
das	**Rathaus, -häuser**	town hall
das	**Restaurant, -s**	restaurant
das	**Schloss, ̈er**	castle
das	**Stadtzentrum, -tren**	city centre, town centre
das	**Straßenschild, -er**	roadsign
das	**Taxi, -s**	taxi
das	**Theater**	theatre
das	**Verkehrsamt, ̈er**	tourist information centre

USEFUL PHRASES

in die Stadt gehen *or* fahren **to go into town**
in der Stadtmitte **in the centre of town**
eine Stadtrundfahrt machen **to go on a tour of the city**
die Straße übergehen **to cross the road**
die Sehenswürdigkeiten besichtigen **to have a look at the sights**

IMPORTANT WORDS (masculine)

der	Betrieb	bustle
der	Bezirk, -e	district
der	Biergarten, ⁝	beer garden
der	Bürgermeister	mayor
der	Einwohner	inhabitant
der	Fahrscheinautomat, -en	ticket machine
der	Fahrscheinentwerter	automatic ticket stamping machine
der	Friedhof, ⁝e	cemetery, graveyard
der	Fußgänger	pedestrian
der	Kreisverkehr	roundabout
der	Platz, ⁝e	square
der	Verkehr	traffic
der	Verkehrsstau, -e	traffic jam
der	Zebrastreifen	zebra crossing

IMPORTANT WORDS (feminine)

die	Aussicht, -en	view
die	Bürgermeisterin	female mayor
die	Feuerwehrwache, -n	fire station
die	Fußgängerzone, -n	pedestrian precinct
die	Menge, -n	crowd
die	Schlange, -n	queue
die	Sehenswürdigkeiten (pl)	sights, places of interest
die	Umgebung, -en	the surroundings (pl)

IMPORTANT WORDS (neuter)

das	Denkmal, ⁝er	monument
das	Fahrzeug, -e	vehicle
das	Gebäude	building
das	Tor, -e	gate(way), arch

USEFUL WORDS *(masculine)*

der	**Abwasserkanal, ̈e**	sewer
der	**Bürger**	citizen
der	**Fußgängerüberweg, -e**	pedestrian crossing
der	**Kinderwagen**	pram
der	**Landkreis, -e**	(like British) county
der	**Marktplatz, ̈e**	market place
der	**Ort, -e**	place, spot
der	**Passant, -en**	passer-by
der	**Pfad, -e**	path
der	**Pflasterstein, -e**	paving stone
der	**Rad(fahr)weg, -e**	cycle path *or* track
der	**Stadtbewohner** *or* der **Städter**	town dweller
der	**Stadtrand, ̈er**	the outskirts *(pl)*
der	**Straßenübergang, ̈e**	pedestrian crossing
der	**Taxistand, ̈e**	taxi rank
der	**Umzug, ̈e**	parade
der	**Wegweiser**	roadsign
der	**Wohnblock, -s**	block of flats
der	**Wolkenkratzer**	skyscraper

USEFUL PHRASES

in der Stadt/am Stadtrand wohnen **to live in the town/in the suburbs**
auf dem Platz **in** *or* **on the square**
an der Ecke **at** *or* **on the corner**
zum Markt gehen, auf den Markt gehen **to go to the market**
Weihnachtsmarkt **Christmas fair**
zu Fuß gehen **to walk**
mit dem Bus/mit dem Zug fahren **to go by bus/by train**
ein Taxi anrufen **to call a taxi**
ins Theater/ins Kino gehen **to go to the theatre/the cinema**
modern **modern**; alt **old**
sauber **clean**; schmutzig **dirty**
typisch **typical**; ziemlich **quite**; sehr **very**

USEFUL WORDS *(feminine)*

die Altstadt	old (part of) town
die Baustelle, -n	building site; roadworks
die Bevölkerung, -en	population
die Gasse, -n	lane, back street
die Großstadt, ¨e	city
die Kreuzung, -en	crossroads
die Kunstgalerie, -n	art gallery
die Leuchtreklame, -n	neon sign
die Meinungsumfrage, -n	opinion poll
die Parkuhr, -en	parking meter
die Prozession, -en	procession
die Sackgasse, -n	dead end
die Siedlung, -en	housing estate
die Sozialwohnung, -en	council flat *or* house
die Spitze, -n	spire
die Stadtmitte, -n	town centre; city centre
die Statue, -n	statue
die Straßenbahn, -en	tram
die Straßenlaterne, -n	street lamp
die Tour, -en	tour
die Umgehungsstraße, -n	by-pass
die Umleitung, -en	diversion
die Vorstadt, ¨e	suburbs *(pl)*

USEFUL WORDS (neuter)

das	**Gedränge**	crowd
das	**Industriegebiet, -e**	industrial area
das	**Kopfsteinpflaster**	cobblestones
das	**Plakat, -e**	poster, notice
das	**Schild, -er**	sign
das	**(Stadt)viertel**	district
das	**Werk, -e**	factory, works
das	**Wohngebiet, -e**	built-up area
das	**Zentrum, -tren**	city centre

USEFUL PHRASES

„Betreten der Baustelle verboten" **"building site: keep out"**

„Anlieger frei" **"residents only"**

„Vorsicht, bissiger Hund!" **"beware of the dog"**

„Fußgängerzone" **"pedestrian precinct"**

„bitte freihalten" **"please keep clear"**

„Parken verboten" **"no parking"**

„Vorfahrt achten!" **"give way"**

ESSENTIAL WORDS *(masculine)*

der	Ausgang, ̈e	exit
der	Ausstieg, -e	exit *(from train)*
der	Bahnhof, ̈e	station
der	Bahnsteig, -e	platform
der	D-Zug, ̈e *(Durchgangszug)*	through train
der	Eilzug, ̈e	limited-stop train
der	Eingang, ̈e	entrance
der	Einstieg, -e	entrance *(onto train)*
der	Entwerter	ticket punching machine
der	Fahrgast, ̈e	passenger
der	Fahrkartenschalter	ticket *or* booking office
der	Fahrschein, -e	ticket
der	Fahrplan, ̈e	timetable
der	Hauptbahnhof, ̈e	main *or* central station
der	Intercity(zug), -s/(̈e)	inter-city train
der	Koffer	case, suitcase
der	Kofferkuli, -s	luggage trolley
der	Nahverkehrszug, ̈e	local train
der	Passagier, -e	passenger
	Reisende(r), -n	traveller
der	Rucksack, ̈e	rucksack, backpack
der	Schnellimbiss, -e	snack bar
der	Schnellzug, ̈e	fast train, express train
der	Speisewagen	dining car
der	U-Bahnhof, ̈e	underground station
der	Wagen	carriage, coach
der	Zug, ̈e	train
der	Zuschlag, ̈e	supplement

ESSENTIAL WORDS *(neuter)*

das	Gepäck	luggage
das	Gleis, -e	platform; track, rails
das	Rad, ̈er	bike
das	Schließfach, ̈er	left luggage locker
das	Taxi, -s	taxi

ESSENTIAL WORDS *(feminine)*

die	**Abfahrt, -en**	departure
die	**Ankunft, ⸚e**	arrival
die	**Auskunft, ⸚e**	information; information desk *or* office
die	**Bahn, -en**	railway
die	**Bahnlinie, -n**	railway line
die	**Brücke, -n**	bridge
	Deutsche Bahn (DB)	German Railways
die	**Einfahrt, -en**	entrance
die	**(einfache) Fahrkarte, (-n) -n**	(single) ticket
die	**Fahrt, -en**	journey
die	**Haltestelle, -n**	stop, station
die	**Klasse, -n**	class
die	**Linie, -n**	line
die	**Reise, -n**	journey
die	**Richtung, -en**	direction
die	**Rückfahrkarte, -n**	return ticket
die	**S-Bahn, -en**	high-speed railway; suburban railway
die	**Station, -en**	station
die	**Tasche, -n**	bag
die	**U-Bahn, -en** *(Untergrundbahn)*	underground (railway)
die	**U-Bahnstation, -en**	underground station
die	**Uhr, -en**	clock; time

USEFUL PHRASES

auf dem Bahnhof **at the station**
sich erkundigen **to make inquiries**
einen Platz reservieren **to book a seat**
nach Bonn einfach **a single to Bonn**
nach Bonn und zurück **a return to Bonn**
zweimal nach Bonn und zurück **two returns to Bonn**
für diese Züge muss man Zuschlag bezahlen **you have to pay a supplement on these trains**
„bitte einsteigen!" **"all aboard"**; „alles aussteigen!" **"all change"**
muss ich umsteigen? **do I have to change trains?**

IMPORTANT WORDS (masculine)

der	Anschluss, ⸚e	connection
der	Dienst, -e	service
der	Dienstwagen	guard's van
der	Eisenbahner	railwayman
der	Fahrausweis, -e	ticket
der	Gepäckwagen	luggage van
der	ICE, -s or der Intercityexpress	high-speed inter-city (train)
der	Liegewagen	couchette
der	Lokomotivführer	train driver
der	Platz, ⸚e	seat
der	Schaffner	guard; ticket collector
der	Schlafwagen	sleeping car, sleeper
der	Zollbeamte, -n	customs officer

IMPORTANT WORDS (feminine)

die	Bahnhofsgaststätte, -n	station buffet
die	Bremse, -n	brake
die	Eisenbahn, -en	railway
die	Gepäckaufbewahrung, -en	left luggage office
die	Grenze, -n	border, frontier
die	Mehrfahrtenkarte, -n	season ticket
die	Notbremse, -n	alarm, communication cord
die	Verbindung, -en	connection
die	Verspätung, -en	delay
die	Zollkontrolle, -n	customs control or check

IMPORTANT WORDS (neuter)

das	Abteil, -e	compartment
das	Fahrgeld, -er	fare
das	Gepäcknetz, -e	luggage rack
das	Nichtraucherabteil, -e	non-smoking compartment
das	Raucherabteil, -e	smoking compartment
das	(Reise)ziel, -e	destination

USEFUL WORDS *(masculine)*

der	**Anhänger**	label, tag
der	**Bahnübergang, ⁀e**	level crossing
der	**Bestimmungsort, -e**	destination *(of goods)*
der	**Fahrpreis, -e**	fare
der	**Gepäckträger**	porter
der	**Güterzug, ⁀e**	goods train
der	**Personenzug, ⁀e**	slow train; passenger train
der	**Pfiff, -e**	whistle
der	**Schrankkoffer**	trunk
der	**Taxistand, ⁀e**	taxi rank
der	**Vorortzug, ⁀e**	commuter train
der	**Wartesaal, -säle**	waiting room

USEFUL WORDS *(feminine)*

die	**Bahncard, -s**	railcard
die	**(Eisenbahn)schienen** *(pl)*	rails
die	**Endstation, -en**	terminus
die	**Entgleisung, -en**	derailment
die	**Lokomotive, -n**	locomotive, engine
die	**Monatskarte, -n**	monthly season ticket
die	**Nummer, -n**	number
die	**Reservierung, -en**	reservation
die	**Rolltreppe, -n**	escalator
die	**Schienen** *(pl)*	rails
die	**Schranke, -n**	level crossing gate
die	**Sperre, -n**	barrier
die	**Strecke, -n**	(section of) railway line *or* track
die	**Wochenkarte, -n**	weekly ticket

USEFUL PHRASES

mit der Bahn **by rail**
den Zug erreichen/verpassen **to catch/miss one's train**
ist dieser Platz frei? **is this seat free?**
hier ist besetzt **this seat is taken**
„nicht hinauslehnen" **"do not lean out of the window"**
verspätet **delayed**

USEFUL WORDS *(feminine)*

die **Beere, -n**	berry
die **Birke, -n**	birch
die **Blutbuche, -n**	copper beech
die **Buche, -n**	beech tree
die **Eibe, -n**	yew
die **Eiche, -n**	oak
die **Esche, -n**	ash
die **Fichte, -n**	spruce, pine
die **Föhre, -n**	Scots pine
die **Kastanie, -n**	chestnut; chestnut tree
die **Kiefer, -n**	pine
die **Knospe, -n**	bud
die **Linde, -n**	lime tree
die **Mistel, -n**	mistletoe
die **Pappel, -n**	poplar
die **Pinie, -n**	pine
die **Platane, -n**	plane tree
die **Rinde, -n**	bark
die **Rosskastanie, -n**	horse chestnut
die **Stechpalme, -n**	holly
die **Tanne, -n**	fir tree
die **Trauerweide, -n**	weeping willow
die **Ulme, -n**	elm
die **Weide, -n**	willow
die **Wurzel, -n**	root

IMPORTANT + USEFUL WORDS *(neuter)*

das **Blatt, ̈-er**	leaf
das **Geäst** *(sg)*	branches
das **Gebüsch** *(sg)*	bushes; undergrowth
das **Holz, ̈-er**	wood *(material)*

USEFUL PHRASES

auf einen Baum klettern **to climb a tree**
im Herbst werden die Blätter gelb **the leaves turn yellow in autumn**
im Schatten eines Baums **in the shade of a tree**

ESSENTIAL + IMPORTANT WORDS *(masculine)*

der Baum, Bäume	tree
der Christbaum, -bäume	Christmas tree
der Forst, -e	forest
der Obstbaum, -bäume	fruit tree
der Obstgarten, ::	orchard
der Schatten	shade, shadow
der Wald, ::er	wood(s), forest
der Weihnachtsbaum, -bäume	Christmas tree

USEFUL WORDS *(masculine)*

der Ahorn, -e	maple
der Ast, ::e	branch
der Buchsbaum, -bäume	box tree
der Busch, ::e	bush, shrub
der Eich(en)baum, -bäume	oak tree
der Kastanienbaum, -bäume	chestnut tree
der Kiefernzapfen	pine cone
der Mistelzweig, -e	(sprig of) mistletoe
der Rotdorn, -e	hawthorn
der Stamm, ::e	trunk
der Strauch, Sträucher	bush, shrub
der Tannenbaum, -bäume	fir tree
der Tannenzapfen	fir cone
der Weidenbaum, -bäume	willow
der Weinberg, -e	vineyard
der Wipfel	tree-top
der Zweig, -e	branch

ESSENTIAL WORDS (*masculine*)

der	Champignon, -s	(button) mushroom
der	Kohl, -e	cabbage
der	Kopfsalat, -e	lettuce
der	Salat, -e	lettuce; salad

IMPORTANT WORDS (*masculine*)

der	Blumenkohl, -e	cauliflower
der	Knoblauch	garlic
der	Pilz, -e	mushroom
der	Rosenkohl	Brussels sprouts (*pl*)
der	Vegetarier	vegetarian

USEFUL WORDS (*masculine*)

der	Gartenkürbis, -se	marrow
der	Kürbis, -se	pumpkin
der	Lauch, -e	leek
der	Mais	sweetcorn
der	Maiskolben	corn on the cob
der	(rote/grüne) Paprika, (-n) -s	(red/green) pepper
der	Porree, -s	leek
der	Rettich, -e	(*large*) radish
der	Rotkohl, -e	red cabbage
der *or* die	Sellerie	celeriac; celery
der	Spargel	asparagus
der	Spinat	spinach
der *or* die	Stangensellerie	celery
der	Weißkohl, -e	white cabbage

USEFUL PHRASES

Gemüse anbauen to grow vegetables; organisch organic
Salzkartoffeln (*pl*) boiled potatoes
Pellkartoffeln (*pl*) potatoes boiled in their jackets
Bratkartoffeln (*pl*) fried *or* sauté potatoes
Knoblauchwurst (*f*) garlic sausage
geraspelte Möhre grated carrot
rot wie eine Tomate as red as a beetroot
vegetarisch vegetarian

ESSENTIAL WORDS *(feminine)*

die	Bohne, -n	bean
die	grüne Bohne, -n -n	French bean
die	Erbse, -n	pea
die	Kartoffel, -n	potato
die	Tomate, -n	tomato
die	Zwiebel, -n	onion

IMPORTANT WORDS *(feminine)*

die	Aubergine, -n	aubergine
die	Avocado, -s	avocado (pear)
die	Brokkoli *(pl)*	broccoli
die	Gurke, -n	cucumber
die	Karotte, -n	carrot
die	Vegetarierin	vegetarian

USEFUL WORDS *(feminine)*

die	Artischocke, -n	artichoke
die	Aubergine, -n	aubergine
die	Brunnenkresse	watercress
die	Endivie, -n	endive
die	Erdartischocke, -n	Jerusalem artichoke
die	Essiggurke, -n	gherkin
die	Kresse	cress
die	Möhre, -n; die Mohrrübe, -n	carrot
die	Paprikaschote, -n	pepper, capsicum
die	Pastinake, -n	parsnip
die	Petersilie	parsley
die	Rübe, -n	turnip
die	Rote Bete *or* Rübe, -n -n	beetroot
die	Zucchini	courgette

ESSENTIAL + IMPORTANT WORDS *(neuter)*

das	Gemüse	vegetable(s)
das	Kraut, Kräuter	herb; cabbage
das	Radieschen	radish
das	Sauerkraut	pickled cabbage

ESSENTIAL WORDS (masculine)

der	Bus, -se	bus
der	Dampfer	steamer
der	Krankenwagen	ambulance
der	Lastkraftwagen (LKW)	lorry, truck; heavy goods vehicle
der	Personenkraftwagen (PKW)	private car
der	Polizeiwagen	police car
der	Straßenbahnwagen	tramcar
der	Tanker	tanker
der	Wagen	car; cart; carriage
der	Wohnwagen	caravan
der	Zug, ¨-e	train

ESSENTIAL WORDS (feminine)

die	Fähre, -n	ferry
die	Straßenbahn, -en	tram
die	U-Bahn, -en	underground

ESSENTIAL WORDS (neuter)

das	Auto, -s	car
das	Boot, -e	boat
das	Fährboot, -e	ferry-boat
das	Fahrrad, ¨-er	bicycle
das	Flugzeug, -e	plane, aeroplane
das	Mofa, -s	moped (small)
das	Motorboot, -e	motorboat
das	Motorrad, ¨-er	motorbike, motorcycle
das	Rad, ¨-er	bike
das	Ruderboot, -e	rowing boat
das	Schiff, -e	ship, vessel
das	Taxi, -s	taxi
das	Wohnmobil, -e	camper, motor caravan

USEFUL PHRASES

reisen **to travel**
fahren **to go**
eine Reise machen **to go on a journey**
gute Reise! **have a good trip!**
mit der Bahn *or* dem Zug fahren **to go by rail** *or* **by train**
mit dem Auto fahren **to drive, go by car**
nach Frankfurt fliegen **to fly to Frankfurt**
zu Fuß gehen **to walk, go on foot**
trampen, per Anhalter fahren **to hitch-hike**
mit einer Höchstgeschwindigkeit von 100 Kilometern pro Stunde fahren
  to drive at a maximum speed of 100 kilometres per hour
seine Fahrkarte entwerten **to cancel one's ticket (in machine)**
Gebrauchtwagen **second-hand cars**
mieten **to hire**
ein Mietauto *(nt)* **a hired car**
öffentliche Verkehrsmittel *(pl)* **public transport**

IMPORTANT WORDS (masculine)

der	Bulldozer	bulldozer
der	Fahrpreis, -e	fare
der	Feuerwehrwagen	fire engine
der	Flugzeugträger	aircraft carrier
der	Hubschrauber	helicopter
der	Jeep, -s	jeep
der	Kindersportwagen	baby buggy, push-chair
der	Lieferwagen	van; delivery van
der	Möbelwagen	removal van, furniture van
der	(Motor)roller	(motor) scooter
der	(Reise)bus, -se	coach
der	Rücksitz, -e	back seat
der	Transporter	van; transporter
der	Vordersitz, -e	front seat

IMPORTANT WORDS (feminine)

die	Autofähre, -n	car ferry
die	fliegende Untertasse, -n -n	flying saucer
die	Gefahr, -en	danger, risk
die	Lokomotive, -n	locomotive, engine

IMPORTANT WORDS (neuter)

das	Fahrgeld, -er	fare
das	Fahrzeug, -e	vehicle
das	Feuerwehrauto, -s	fire engine
das	Kanu, -s	canoe
das	Moped, -s	moped
das	Raumschiff, -e	spaceship
das	Rettungsboot, -e	lifeboat
das	Schnellboot, -e	speedboat
das	Segelboot, -e	sailing boat
das	UFO, -s	UFO (unidentified flying object)

USEFUL WORDS (masculine)

der	Anhänger	trailer
der	Karren	cart
der	Kinderwagen	pram
der	Kombiwagen	estate car, station wagon
der	Lastkahn, -e	barge
der	(Luft)ballon, -s or -e	balloon
der	Omnibus, -se	bus
der	Panzer	tank
der	Sattelschlepper	articulated lorry
der	Schleppdampfer; der Schlepper	tug, tugboat
der	Sessellift, -e or -s	chairlift
der	Streifenwagen	(police) patrol car
der	Vergnügungsdampfer	pleasure steamer

USEFUL WORDS (feminine)

die	Dampfwalze, -n	steamroller
die	Drahtseilbahn, -en	cable railway, funicular
die	Düse, -n	jet (plane)
die	Jacht, -en	yacht
die	Planierraupe, -n	bulldozer
die	Rakete, -n	rocket
die	Schwebebahn, -en	cable or overhead railway

USEFUL WORDS (neuter)

das	Düsenflugzeug, -e	jet plane
das	Luftkissenboot, -e	hovercraft
das	Paddelboot, -e	canoe
das	Schlauchboot, -e	inflatable dinghy
das	Segelflugzeug, -e	glider
das	Tankschiff, -e	tanker
das	Transportmittel	means of transport (goods)
das	U-Boot, -e (Unterseeboot)	submarine
das	Verkehrsmittel	means of transport (passengers)

ESSENTIAL WORDS *(masculine)*

der	Abend, -e	evening
der	Berg, -e	mountain
der	Blitz, -e	(flash of) lightning
der	Donner	thunder
der	Frost, ¨-e	frost
der	Frühling, -e	spring
der	Grad, -e	degree
der	Herbst, -e	autumn
der	Himmel	sky; heaven
der	Monat, -e	month
der	Morgen	morning
der	Nachmittag, -e	afternoon
der	Nebel	fog, mist
der	Nord(en)	north
der	Ort, -e *or* ¨-er	place
der	Osten	east
der	Regen	rain
der	Schnee	snow
der	Schneesturm, ¨-e	snowstorm
der	Sommer	summer
der	Sonnenschein	sunshine
der	Sturm, ¨-e	storm, gale; tempest
der	Süden	south
der	Westen	west
der	Wind, -e	wind
der	Winter	winter

USEFUL PHRASES

blitzen **to flash** (es blitzt); donnern **to thunder** (es donnert)
frieren **to freeze** (es friert); gießen **to pour** (es gießt)
nieseln **to drizzle** (es nieselt); regnen **to rain** (es regnet)
scheinen **to shine** (die Sonne scheint)
schneien **to snow** (es schneit)
es fängt an zu schneien **it's beginning to snow**

ESSENTIAL WORDS *(feminine)*

die	**Insel, -n**	island
die	**Jahreszeit, -en**	season
die	**Luft**	air
die	**Nacht, ⁻e**	night
die	**Natur**	nature
die	**Sonne**	sun
die	**Temperatur, -en**	temperature
die	**Welt**	world
die	**Wolke, -n**	cloud

ESSENTIAL WORDS *(neuter)*

das	**Eis**	ice
das	**Gewitter**	thunderstorm
das	**Glatteis**	black ice
das	**Jahr, -e**	year
das	**Land, ⁻er**	country
das	**Licht, -er**	light
das	**Wetter**	weather

USEFUL PHRASES

wie ist das Wetter heute? **what's the weather like today?**
wie ist das Wetter bei euch? **what's the weather like with you?**
wie ist die Wettervorhersage? **what's the weather forecast?**
heiß **hot**; kalt **cold**
warm **warm**; kühl **cool**
herrlich **marvellous**; schön **lovely**; schrecklich **terrible**
sonnig **sunny**; windig **windy**
mild **mild**; rau **harsh**
schwül **sultry, close**; trüb **dull**
bedeckt **overcast**; bewölkt **cloudy**
stürmisch **stormy**; neblig **misty**
trocken **dry**; nass **wet**; feucht **damp**
heiter **bright**; regnerisch **rainy**

IMPORTANT WORDS *(masculine)*

der **Donnerschlag**, ¨e	thunderclap
der **Hagel**	hail
der **Mond**	moon
der **Mondschein**	moonlight
der **Niederschlag**, ¨e	rainfall, precipitation
der **Planet**, -en	planet
der **Regenschauer**	shower of rain
der **(Regen)schirm**, -e	umbrella
der **Regentropfen**	raindrop
der **Schatten**	shadow; shade
der **Schauer**	shower
der **Schneefall**, ¨e	snowfall
der **Schneeregen**	sleet
der **Smog**	smog
der **Sonnenschirm**, -e	parasol, sunshade
der **Stern**, -e	star
der **Wetterbericht**, -e	weather report

IMPORTANT WORDS *(feminine)*

die **Front**, -en	front
die **Hitze**	heat
die **Kälte**	cold
die **Verbesserung**, -en	improvement
die **Wetterlage**	weather situation
die **Wettervorhersage**, -n	weather forecast

IMPORTANT WORDS *(neuter)*

das **Halbdunkel**	semi-darkness
das **Klima**, -s *or* -ta	climate
das **Mondlicht**	moonlight
das **Sauwetter**	awful weather

USEFUL PHRASES

herrschen to prevail; zeitweise for a time
vereinzelt bewölkt with (occasional) cloudy patches
plus plus; minus minus
so ein Sauwetter! what awful weather!

USEFUL WORDS (masculine)

der	Blitzableiter	lightning conductor
der	Dunst	haze
der	Eiszapfen	icicle
der	Gefrierpunkt	freezing point
der	Hochdruck	high pressure
der	Orkan, ̈e	hurricane
der	Platzregen	downpour
der	Regenbogen	rainbow
der	Sonnenaufgang, ̈e	sunrise
der	Sonnenstrahl, -en	ray of sunshine
der	Sonnenuntergang, ̈e	sunset
der	Tagesanbruch	dawn, break of day
der	Tau	dew
der	Tiefdruck	low pressure
der	Windstoß, ̈e	gust of wind

USEFUL WORDS (feminine)

die	Atmosphäre	atmosphere
die	Aufheiterungen (pl)	bright periods
die	Bö, -en	squall, gust of wind
die	Brise, -n	breeze
die	Dürre, -n	(period of) drought
die	Flut, -en	flood
die	Hitzewelle, -n	heat wave
die	Kältewelle, -n	cold spell
die	(Morgen)dämmerung, -en	dawn
die	Schneeflocke, -n	snowflake
die	Schneewehe, -n	snowdrift
die	Überschwemmung, -en	flood, deluge

USEFUL WORDS (neuter)

das	Barometer	barometer
das	Schneegestöber	flurry of snow
das	Tauwetter	thaw
das	Unwetter	thunderstorm
das	Zwielicht	twilight

ESSENTIAL WORDS (masculine)

der	Ausweis, -e	card
der	Empfang, ̈-e	reception
der	Herbergsvater, ̈-	warden
der	Junge, -n	boy
der	Rucksack, ̈-e	backpack, rucksack
der	Schlafsack, ̈-e	sleeping bag
der	Spaziergang, ̈-e	walk
der	Speisesaal, -säle	dining room
der	Stadtplan, ̈-e	street map
der	Urlaub, -e	holiday(s)

ESSENTIAL WORDS (feminine)

die	Anmeldung, -en	registration
die	Dusche, -n	shower
die	Herbergsmutter, ̈-	(female) warden
die	Jugendherberge, -n	youth hostel
die	Küche, -n	kitchen
die	Landkarte, -n	map
die	Mahlzeit, -en	meal
die	Toilette, -n	toilet
die	Übernachtung, -en	overnight stay

ESSENTIAL WORDS (neuter)

das	Abendessen	dinner, evening meal
das	Badezimmer	bathroom
das	Bett, -en	bed
das	Büro, -s	office
das	Essen	food; meal
das	Frühstück, -e	breakfast
das	Mädchen	girl

USEFUL PHRASES

bleiben to stay
übernachten to spend the night
sich anmelden to register
mieten to hire
„Hausordnung für Jugendherbergen" "youth hostel rules"

IMPORTANT WORDS *(masculine)*

der	Aufenthalt, -e	stay
	Erwachsene(r), -n	adult
der	Feuerlöscher	fire extinguisher
	Jugendliche(r), -n	young person
der	Mülleimer	dustbin
der	Prospekt, -e	leaflet, brochure
der	Reiseführer	guidebook
der	Schlafsaal, -säle	dormitory
der	Waschraum, -räume	washroom
der	Waschsalon, -s	laundrette
der	Zimmernachweis, -e	accommodation office

IMPORTANT WORDS *(feminine)*

die	Bettwäsche	bed linen, bedclothes *(pl)*
die	Mitgliedskarte, -n	membership card
die	Nachtruhe	lights-out
die	Ruhe	quiet
die	Unterkunft, -künfte	accommodation
die	Veranstaltung, -en	organization
die	Wäsche	washing *(things)*

IMPORTANT WORDS *(neuter)*

das	Etagenbett, -en	bunk bed
das	schwarze Brett, -n -er	notice board

The vocabulary items on pages 206 to 229 have been grouped under parts of speech rather than topics because they can apply in a wide range of circumstances. Use them just as freely as the vocabulary already given.

ADJECTIVES

> **What is an adjective?**
> An **adjective** is a 'describing' word that tells you more about a person or thing, such as their appearance, colour, size or other qualities, for example, *pretty*, *blue*, *big*.

abgenutzt worn out (*object*)
abscheulich hideous
ähnlich (+ *dat*) similar (to), like
aktuell topical
albern silly, foolish
allerlei all kinds of
allgemein general
alltäglich ordinary; daily
alt old
amüsant amusing
andere(r, s) other
anders different
angenehm pleasant
angrenzend neighbouring
arm poor
artig well-behaved, good
aufgeregt excited
aufgeweckt bright, lively
aufrichtig sincere
ausführlich detailed, elaborate
ausgestreckt stretched (out)
ausgezeichnet excellent
ausschließlich sole, exclusive
außerordentlich extra-ordinary
befriedigend satisfactory
begeistert keen, enthusiastic
belebt busy (*street*)

beleuchtet illuminated
beliebt popular
bemerkenswert remarkable
benachbart neighbouring
bereit ready
berühmt famous
beschäftigt (mit) busy (with) (*of person*)
besetzt engaged; taken
besondere(r, s) special
besorgt worried, anxious
besser better
betrunken drunk
beunruhigt worried, disturbed
blöd silly, stupid
brav well-behaved
breit wide, broad
bunt colourful
dankbar grateful
dauernd perpetual, constant
delikat delicate; delicious
deutlich clear; distinct
dicht thick, dense
dick thick
doof daft, stupid
dreckig dirty, filthy
dringend urgent

dumm silly, stupid; annoying
dunkel dark
dünn thin
dynamisch dynamic
echt real, genuine
ehemalig old, former
ehrlich sincere, honest
eifrig keen, enthusiastic
eigen own
einfach simple; single
einzeln single, individual
einzig only
elegant elegant, smart
elektrisch, Elektro- electric
elend poor, wretched
End-final
endgültig final, definite
endlos endless
eng narrow; tight
entschlossen firm, determined
entsetzlich dreadful
entzückend delightful
erfahren experienced
ernst serious, solemn
ernsthaft serious, earnest
erreichbar reachable, within reach
erschöpft exhausted, worn out
erste(r, s) first
erstaunlich amazing,
  extraordinary
erstaunt astonished
fähig (zu) capable (of)
falsch false; wrong
faul rotten; lazy
feierlich solemn
fein fine
fern far-off, distant
fertig prepared, ready
fest firm, hard

fett fat; greasy
finster dark
flach flat
fortgeschritten advanced
fortwährend continual, endless
frech cheeky
frei free, vacant
frisch fresh
furchtbar frightful
fürchterlich terrible, awful
ganz whole, complete
geduldig patient
geeignet suitable
gefährlich dangerous
gefroren frozen
geheim secret
geheimnisvoll mysterious
gemischt mixed
gemütlich comfortable
genau exact, precise
gerade straight; even
geringste(r, s) slightest, least
gesamt whole, entire
geschichtlich historical
gestattet allowed
gewaltig tremendous, huge
gewalttätig violent
gewiss certain
gewöhnlich usual; ordinary;
  common
glatt smooth
gleich same; equal
glücklich happy; fortunate
gnädig gracious
gnädige Frau Madam
graziös graceful
grob coarse, rude
groß big, great, large; tall
großartig magnificent

günstig suitable, convenient
gut good
hart hard
hässlich ugly
Haupt- main
heftig fierce, violent
heiß hot
hell pale; bright, light
herrlich marvellous
hervorragend excellent
historisch historical
hoch high
höflich polite, civil
hübsch pretty
intelligent intelligent
interessant interesting
jede(r, s) each, every
jung young
kalt cold
kein no, not any
klar clear, sharp
klatschnass soaking wet
klein small, little
klug wise, clever
komisch funny
kompliziert complicated
körperlich physical
kostbar expensive; precious
kostenlos free (of charge)
köstlich delicious
kräftig strong
kühl cool
kurz short
lächelnd smiling
lächerlich ridiculous
lahm lame
Landes- national
lang long; tall (*of person*)
langsam slow

langweilig boring
laut loud, noisy
lebendig alive; lively
lebhaft lively (*of person*)
lecker delicious, tasty
leer empty
leicht easy; light (*weight*)
leidenschaftlich passionate
leise quiet; soft
letzte(r, s) last, latest; final
lieb dear
Lieblings- favourite
linke(r, s) left
lustig amusing; cheerful
sich lustig machen über (*+ acc*)
   to make fun of
luxuriös luxurious
Luxus- luxury, luxurious
mächtig powerful, mighty
mager thin
mehrere several
merkwürdig strange, odd
Militär-, militärisch military
mindeste(r, s) least
mitleidig sympathetic
modern modern
möglich possible
müde tired
munter lively
mutig courageous
mysteriös mysterious
nächste(r, s) next; nearest
nah(e) near; close
natürlich natural
nett nice, kind
neu new
neugierig curious
niedrig low
nötig necessary

notwendig necessary
nützlich useful
nutzlos useless
obligatorisch compulsory, obligatory
offen open; frank, sincere
offenbar, offensichtlich obvious
öffentlich public
offiziell official
ordentlich (neat and) tidy
Orts- local
pädagogisch educational
passend suitable
persönlich personal
• populär popular
prächtig magnificent
privat private; personal
privilegiert privileged
pünktlich punctual
Quadrat-, quadratisch square
rau rough; harsh
rechte(r, s) right
reich rich
reif ripe
rein clean
reizend charming
religiös religious
reserviert reserved
richtig right, correct
riesig huge, gigantic
romantisch romantic
ruhig quiet, peaceful
rund round
sanft gentle, soft
satt full (person)
ich habe es satt I'm fed up (with it)
sauber clean
scharf sharp; spicy
schattig shady

scheu shy
schick smart, chic
schläfrig sleepy
schlank slender, slim
schlau cunning, sly
schlecht bad
schlimm bad
schmal narrow; slender
schmutzig dirty
schnell fast, quick, rapid
schön beautiful
schrecklich terrible; frightful
schroff steep; jagged; brusque
schüchtern shy
schwach weak
schweigsam silent
schwer heavy; serious
schwierig difficult
seltsam strange, odd, curious
sicher sure; safe
sichtbar visible
solche(r, s) such
Sonder- special
sonderbar strange, odd
sorgenfrei carefree
sorgfältig careful
spannend exciting
Stadt-, städtisch municipal, urban
ständig perpetual
stark strong; heavy
steif stiff
steil steep
still quiet, still
stolz (auf + acc) proud (of)
streng severe, harsh; strict
stur stubborn
süß sweet
sympathisch likeable
tapfer brave

technisch technical
tief deep
toll mad; terrific
tot dead
tragbar portable
traurig sad
treu true (*friend etc*)
trocken dry
typisch typical
übel wicked, bad
übrig left-over
unartig naughty
unbekannt unknown
uneben uneven
unerträglich unbearable
ungeheuer huge
ungezogen rude
unglaublich incredible
unglücklich unhappy; unfortunate
unheimlich weird
unmöglich impossible
ursprünglich original
verantwortlich responsible
verboten prohibited, forbidden
verlegen embarrassed
verletzt injured
verliebt in love

vernünftig sensible, reasonable
verrückt mad, crazy
verschieden various; different
verständlich understandable
viereckig square
volkstümlich popular (*of the people*)
voll (+ *gen*) full (of)
vollkommen perfect, complete
vollständig complete
vorderste(r, s) front (*row etc*)
wach awake
wahr true
warm warm
weich soft
weise wise
weit wide
wert worth
wichtig important
wild fierce, wild
wohlhabend well-off
wunderbar wonderful, marvellous
zäh tough
zahlreich numerous
zart gentle, tender
zig umpteen
zufrieden satisfied, contented
zusätzlich extra

ADVERBS

> **What is an adverb?**
> An **adverb** is a word usually used with verbs, adjectives or other adverbs that gives more information about when, how, where, or in what circumstances something happens: *quickly, happily, now* are all adverbs.

Many other adverbs have the same form as the adjective.

absichtlich deliberately, on purpose
allein alone, on one's own some day
allerdings certainly; of course, to be sure
am besten best, best of all
am liebsten most (of all), best (of all)
am meisten (the) most
anders otherwise; differently
auf einmal all at once
äußerst extremely, most
bald soon; almost
besonders especially, particularly
bestimmt definitely, for sure
bloß only, merely
da there; here; then
daher from there; from that
dahin (to) there; then
damals at that time
danach after that; afterwards
dann then
darin in it, in there
deshalb therefore, for that reason
doch after all
dort there
dorthin (to) there
draußen out of doors; outside
drinnen inside; indoors
drüben over there, on the other side

durchaus thoroughly, absolutely
eben exactly; just
eher sooner; rather
eigentlich really, actually
einmal once; one day,
endlich at last, finally
erst first; only (*time*)
erstens first(ly), in the first place
etwa about; perhaps
fast almost, nearly
früh early
ganz quite; completely
gar nicht not at all
gegenwärtig at present, at the moment
genau exactly, precisely
genug enough
gerade just, exactly
geradeaus straight ahead
gern(e) willingly; gladly
gewöhnlich usually
glücklicherweise fortunately
gut well
häufig frequently
heutzutage nowadays
hier here
hierher this way, here
hin und her to and fro
hinten at the back, behind

höchst highly, extremely
hoffentlich I hope, hopefully
immer always
immer noch still
inzwischen meanwhile, in the meantime
irgendwo(hin) (to) somewhere
je ... desto: je mehr desto besser the more the better
je ever
jedenfalls in any case
jedesmal each time, everytime
jedesmal wenn whenever
jemals ever; at any time
jetzt now
kaum hardly, scarcely
keineswegs in no way; by no means
komischerweise funnily (enough), in a funny way
künftig in future
lange for a long time
langsam slowly
lauter (with pl) nothing but, only
leider unfortunately
lieber rather, preferably
links left; on or to the left
manchmal sometimes
mehr more
meinetwegen for my sake; on my account
meistens mostly, for the most part
mitten (in) in the middle or midst (of)
möglichst as ... as possible
nachher afterwards
natürlich naturally
neu füllen etc to refill etc
neu newly; afresh, anew

nicht not
nichtsdestoweniger nevertheless
nie, niemals never
noch einmal (once) again
noch still; yet
normalerweise normally
nun now
nur just, only
oben above; upstairs
oft often
plötzlich suddenly
rechts right; on or to the right
richtig correctly; really
rundherum round about, all (a)round
schlecht badly
schließlich finally
schnell quickly
schon already
sehr very, a lot, very much
selbst even
selten seldom, rarely
so so, thus, like this
sofort at once, immediately
sogar even
sogleich at once, straight away
sonst otherwise; or else
spät late
überall(hin) everywhere
übrigens besides, by the way
umher about, around
ungefähr about, approximately
unten below; downstairs; at the bottom
unterwegs on the way
viel much, a lot
vielleicht perhaps, maybe
völlig completely
vorbei by, past

vorher before, previously, beforehand

wahrscheinlich probably

wann(?) when(?)

warum(?) why(?)

weit far

wie(?), wie! how(?), how!

wieder again

wirklich really

wo/woher/wohin/wovon(?) where/from where/(to) where/from where(?)

ziemlich fairly, rather

zu to

zuerst first; at first

zufällig by chance; by any chance

zurück back

zweitens second(ly), in the second place

SOME MORE NOUNS

> **What is a noun?**
> A **noun** is a 'naming' word for a living being, thing or idea, for example, *woman, Andrew, desk, happiness*.

das Abenteuer adventure
der Abhang, ⸚e slope
die Abkürzung, -en abbreviation; short-cut
der Abschnitt, -e section
die Absicht, -en intention
der Abstieg, -e descent
die Abteilung, -en department, section
die Abwesenheit, -en absence
die Ahnung, -en idea, suspicion
die Änderung, -en alteration, change
der Anfang, ⸚e beginning
zu Anfang at the beginning
die Angst, ⸚e fear
ich habe Angst (vor + *dat*) I am afraid *or* frightened (of)
die Anmeldung, -en announcement
die Anstalten (*fpl*) preparations
die Anstrengung, -en effort
die Antwort, -en answer, reply
die Anweisungen (*fpl*) orders, instructions
die Anwesenheit presence
das Anzeichen sign, indication
die Anzeige, -n advertisement
der Apparat, -e machine
das Ärgernis, -se annoyance
die Art, -en way, method; kind, sort
auf meine Art in my own way
aller Art of all kinds
der Aufenthalt, -e stay

die Aufmerksamkeit attention; attentiveness
die Aufsicht supervision
der Aufstieg, -e ascent
der Ausdruck, ⸚e term, expression
die Auseinandersetzung, -en argument
der Ausgangspunkt, -e starting point
die Ausnahme, -n exception
die Ausstellung, -en exhibition
die Auswahl, -en (an + *dat*) selection (of)
der Bau construction
die Beaufsichtigung supervision
die Bedeutung, -en meaning; importance
die Bedingung, -en condition, stipulation
das Bedürfnis, -se need
der Befehl, -e order, command
die Begabung, -en talent
der Begriff: im Begriff sein, etw zu tun to be about to do sth
das Beispiel, -e example
zum Beispiel for example
die Bemerkung, -en remark
die Bemühung, -en trouble, effort
die Berechnung, -en calculation
der Bescheid, -e message, information
jdm Bescheid sagen to let sb know

sein Bestes tun to do one's best
der Betrag, ⸚e sum, amount
(of money)
der Blödsinn nonsense
die Botschaft, -en message, news;
embassy
die Breite, -n width
der Bursche, -n fellow
die Chance, -n chance, opportunity
der Dank thanks (pl)
die Darstellung, -en portrayal,
representation
das Denken thinking, thought
das Diagramm, -e diagram
die Dicke, -n thickness; fatness
der Dienst, -e service
die Dimension -en dimension
das Ding, -e thing, object
der Duft, ⸚e smell, fragrance
die Dummheit, -en stupidity;
stupid mistake
der Dummkopf, ⸚e idiot
der Dunst, ⸚e vapour
die Ecke, -n corner
die Ehre, -n honour
die Einbildung, -en imagination
der Eindruck, ⸚e impression
der Einfall, ⸚e thought, idea
die Einzelheit, -en detail
die Eleganz elegance
der Empfang, ⸚e reception
die Empfindung, -en feeling,
emotion
das Ende, -n end
zu Ende gehen to end
die Entschlossenheit resolution,
determination
das Ereignis, -se event
die Erfahrung, -en experience

der Erfolg, -e result; success
das Ergebnis, -se result
die Erinnerung, -en memory,
remembrance
die Erklärung, -en explanation
die Erkundigung, -en inquiry
die Erlaubnis, -se permission; permit
das Erlebnis, -se experience
der Ernst seriousness
im Ernst in earnest
das Erstaunen astonishment
die Erwiderung, -en retort
das Exil, -e exile (state)
der Feind, -e enemy
die Flamme, -n flame
die Folge, -n order; series; result
die Form, -en form, shape
die Frage, -n question
Fremde(r), -n, die Fremde, -n
stranger; foreigner
die Freude, -n joy, delight
die Freundlichkeit, -en kindness
die Freundschaft, -en friendship
der Frieden peace
die Frische freshness
der Führer guide; leader
die Gebühr, -en fee, charge
das Gedächtnis, -se memory
der Gedanke, -n thought
die Geduld patience
die Gefahr, -en danger
der Gegenstand, ⸚e object
das Gegenteil, -e opposite
im Gegenteil on the contrary
die Gegenwart present
das Geheimnis, -se mystery; secret
die Gelegenheit, -en opportunity,
occasion
das Gerät, -e device, tool

das Geräusch, -e sound, noise
der Geruch, -̈e smell
das Geschick, -e fate; skill
der Geselle, -n fellow
der Gesichtspunkt, -e point of view
das Glück luck; happiness
der Gott, -̈er god
der (liebe) Gott God
der Grund, -̈e reason
die Gruppe, -n group
die Grüße (mpl) wishes
die Güte kindness
die Hauptsache, -n the main thing
der Heimweg, -e way home
die Herstellung, -en manufacture
die Hilfe help
der Hintergrund, -̈e background
die Hoffnung, -en hope
die Höflichkeit, -en politeness
die Höhe, -n height; level
die Idee, -n idea
das Interesse, -n interest
der Kampf, -̈e fight, battle
die Kapelle, -n chapel
das Kapitel chapter
die Katastrophe, -n disaster, catastrophe
die Kenntnis, -se knowledge
der Kerl, -e fellow, chap
die Kette, -n chain
der Klang, -̈e sound
die Klimaanlage air conditioning
der Kollege, -n, die Kollegin colleague
die Konstruktion, -en construction
die Kontrolle, -n control, supervision
die Kopie, -n copy

der Korb, -̈e basket
die Kosten (pl) cost(s); expenses
der Kreis, -e circle; district
der Krieg, -e war
der Kurort, -e health resort
der Kuss, -̈e kiss
das Lächeln smile
die Lage, -n situation
die Länge, -n length
die Lang(e)weile boredom
der Lärm noise
der Laut, -e sound
das Leben life
der Lebenslauf, -̈e CV
das Leid sorrow, grief
der Leiter chief, leader
der Leser, die Leserin reader
das Licht, -er light
die Liebe, -n love
die Linie, -n line
die Liste, -n list
die Literatur literature
das Loch, -̈er hole
die Lösung, -en solution
die Lücke, -n opening, gap
die Lüge, -n lie
die Lust: ich habe Lust, es zu tun I feel like doing it
die Macht, -̈e power
das Magazin, -e magazine
der Mangel, -̈e (an + dat) lack (of), shortage (of)
die Maschine, -n machine
das Maximum, -a maximum
die Meinung, -en opinion, view
meiner Meinung nach in my opinion
das meiste; die meisten most
die Meldung, -en announcement

die Menge, -n crowd; quantity, lot

das Minimum, -a minimum

die Mischung, -en mixture

das Missgeschick, -e misfortune

das Mitleid sympathy

die Mitteilung, -en communication

das Mittel means; method

das Modell, -e model, version

die Möglichkeit, -en means; possibility

sein Möglichstes tun to doone's best

die Mühe, -n pains, trouble

die Münze, -n coin

der Mut courage, spirit

die Nachrichten (fpl) news; information

der Nachteil, -e disadvantage

die Nähe: in der Nähe close by

das Netz, -e network

die Not need, distress

die Notiz, -en note, item

die Nummer, -n number

das Objekt, -e object

die Öffentlichkeit the general public

die Öffnung, -en opening

die Ordnung, -en order

in Ordnung bringen to arrange, tidy (up)

alles ist in Ordnung everything is all right

der Ort, -e place

das Pech misfortune, bad luck

der Pfeil, -e arrow

das Pfund, -e pound (sterling); pound (weight)

der Plan, ¨-e plan; map

der Platz, ¨-e place; seat; room, space; square

die Politik politics; policy

das Porträt, -s portrait

das Problem, -e problem

das Produkt, -e product; produce

der Punkt, -e point; dot; full stop

die Puppe, -n doll

die Qualität, -en quality

der Radau hullaballoo

der Rand, ¨-er edge; rim

der Rat, -schläge (piece of) advice

das Rätsel puzzle, riddle

der Rauch smoke

der Raum, Räume space; room

das Recht, -e law; justice; right

Recht haben to be right

die Rede, -n speech

eine Rede halten to make a speech

die Regierung, -en government; reign

die Reihe, -n series; line

ich bin an der Reihe it's my turn now

der Reiz, -e attraction, charm

die Reklame, -n advertisement

der Rest remainder, rest

die Reste (mpl) remains

das Resultat, -e result

der Revolutionär, -e revolutionary

der Rhythmus, -men rhythm

die Richtung, -en direction

die Rückseite, -n back (of page etc)

der Ruf, -e call, cry; reputation

die Ruhe rest; peace; calm; silence

die Sache, -n thing; matter

der Schein, -e (bank) note

ein 20-Mark-Schein a 20-mark note

das Schicksal, -e fate

das Schild, -er sign; label

der Schlag, ⸚e blow, knock
der Schluss, ⸚e end(ing)
am Schluss at the end
der Schmutz, die Schmutzigkeit
dirt, dirtiness
der Schrei, -e cry, scream
der Schritt, -e footstep; step, pace
die Schuld fault
ich bin nicht schuld daran it's not
my fault
die Schwierigkeit, -en difficulty
die Sensation, -en stir, sensation
die Serie, -n series
die Sicherheit, -en security; safety
die Sicht sight; view
der Sieg, -e victory
der Sinn, -e mind; sense; meaning
die Situation, -en situation
die Sorge, -n care, worry
sich (dat) Sorgen machen to be
worried
die Sorte, -n sort, kind
das Souvenir, -s souvenir
der Spalt crack, opening; split
die Spalte, -n column (of page)
der Spaß, ⸚e fun; joke
der Spektakel hullaballo
das Spielzeug, -e toy
die Spur, -en sign, trace
der Staat, -en state
der Standpunkt, -e point of view,
standpoint
die Stärke, -n power, strength
die Stelle, -n place
die Steuer, -n tax
der Stil, -e style
die Stille quietness
die Stimmung, -en mood;
atmosphere

die Strecke, -n stretch; distance
das Stück, -e piece, part
die Summe, -n sum
das System, -e system
das Talent, -e talent
in der Tat in (actual) fact, indeed
die Tätigkeit, -en activity
der Teil, -e, das Teil, -e part, section
der Text, -e text
der Titel title
die Tiefe, -n depth
der Traum, ⸚e dream
der Treffpunkt, -e meeting place
der Trost comfort
die Trümmer (pl) wreckage; ruins
der Typ, -en type
Überlebende(r), -n survivor
die Überraschung, -en surprise
die Umgebung, -en surroundings
(pl)
das Unglück, -e misfortune;
bad luck; disaster
das Unheil evil; disaster,
misfortune
das Unrecht: Unrecht haben to be
wrong, be mistaken
die Unterbrechung, -en
interruption
die Unterhaltung, -en
conversation, chat
das Unternehmen undertaking,
enterprise
der Unterschied, -e difference
der Urlaub, -e holidays, leave
die Ursache, -n reason, cause
die Verabredung, -en appointment
die Verbindung, -en connection
der Vergleich, -e comparison
das Vergnügen pleasure

der Versuch, -e attempt
das Vertrauen confidence
die Vorbereitung, -en preparation
der Vorschlag, ⁓e suggestion
die Vorsicht care, caution
die Vorstellung, -en introduction;
   idea, thought
der Vorteil, -e advantage
die Wahl, -en choice, selection;
   election
der Wähler voter
die Wahrheit, -en truth
der Wechselkurs, -e exchange rate
die Weile, -n while
die Weise, -n way, method, manner
auf diese Weise in this way *or*
   manner
die Weite, -n width; distance
die Werbung, -en advertising
der Wert, -e value
die Wette, -n bet

die Wichtigkeit importance
die Wirklichkeit, -en fact, reality
die Wirkung, -en effect
der Witz, -e joke
der Wohlstand prosperity
das Wort, ⁓er *or* -e word
der Wunsch, ⁓e wish
die Wut rage, fury
die Zahl, -en number, figure
das Zeichen sign
die Zeile, -n line *(of text)*
die Zeitschrift, -en magazine
die Zeitung, -en newspaper
das Zentrum, Zentren centre
das Zeug stuff; gear
das Ziel, -e aim, goal; destination
das Ziffer, -n number, figure
der Zorn anger
die Zutaten *(pl)* ingredients
der Zweck, -e purpose

PREPOSITIONS AND CONJUNCTIONS

What is a preposition?
A preposition is one word such as *at*, *for*, *with*, *into* or *from*, or words such as *in front of* or *near to*, which are usually followed by a noun or a pronoun or, in English, a word ending in *-ing*.

Prepositions show how people and things relate to the rest of the sentence, for example, *She's at home; It's for you; You'll get into trouble; It's in front of you*.

What is a conjunction?
A conjunction is a word such as *and*, *but*, *or*, *so*, *if* and *because*, that links two words or phrases of a similar type, or two parts of a sentence, for example, *Diane and I have been friends for years; I left because I was bored*.

aber but; however
als when; as; than
als ob, als wenn as if, as though
also therefore, so
anstatt (+ *gen*) instead of
außer (+ *dat*) out of; except
außerhalb (+ *gen*) outside
bei (+ *dat*) near, by; at the house of
bevor before (*time*)
bis until, till (*conj*); (+ *acc*) until; (up) to, as far as
da as, since, seeing (that)
damit so that, in order that
dass that
denn for
ehe before
entweder ... oder either... or
gegenüber (+ *dat*) opposite; to(wards)
gerade als just as
hinter (+ *dat or acc*) behind
indem es, while
innerhalb (+ *gen*) in(side), within

je ..., desto the more ... the more
nachdem after
nun (da) now (that)
ob if, whether
obwohl although
oder or
ohne dass without
seit (+ *dat*) since
sobald as soon as
sodass so that
solange as long as
sondern (*after neg*) but
nicht nur ... sondern auch not only ... but also
sowohl ... als (auch) both... and
statt (+ *gen*) instead of
stattdessen instead
teils ... teils partly ... partly
trotz (+ *gen*) despite, in spite of
und and
während while (*conj*); (+ *gen*) during (*prep*)
weder ... noch neither ... nor

wegen (*+ gen*) because of
weil because
wenn when; if

wenn ... auch although; even if
wie as, like

VERBS

What is a verb?
A **verb** is a 'doing' word which describes what somebody or something does, what they are, or what happens to them, for example, *play*, *be*, *disappear*.

abhängen von to depend on
abholen to fetch, go and meet
  (*somebody*)
ablehnen to refuse
abnehmen to lose weight
abschreiben to copy
akzeptieren to accept
anbeten to adore
anbieten to give, offer
anblicken to look (at)
ändern: seine Meinung ändern
  to change one's mind
anfangen to begin
angeben to state
angehören (+ *dat*) to belong to
  (*club etc*)
angreifen to attack; to touch
anhalten to stop; to continue
ankommen to arrive
ankündigen to announce
annehmen to accept; to assume
anschalten to switch on
antworten to answer, reply
anzeigen to announce
anziehen to attract; to put (on)
  (*clothes*)
sich ärgern to get angry
atmen to breathe
aufbewahren to keep, store
aufhängen to hang (up)
aufheben to raise, lift

aufhören to stop
aufkleben to stick on *or* onto
aufmachen to open
aufpassen (auf + *acc*) to watch;
  to be careful (of)
aufstehen to get up
aufwachen to wake up (*intransitive*)
aufwärmen to warm (up)
aufwecken to awaken, wake up
  (*transitive*)
ausdrücken to express
ausführen to carry out, execute
ausgeben to spend (*money*)
ausleihen to borrow
auslöschen to put out, extinguish
ausrufen to exclaim, cry (out)
sich ausruhen to rest
ausschalten to switch off
ausschlafen to have a good sleep
aussprechen to pronounce
ausstrecken to extend, hold out
sich ausstrecken to stretch out
auswählen to select
beabsichtigen to intend
beachten to observe, obey
sich (bei jdm) bedanken to say
  thank you (to sb)
bedauern to regret
bedecken to cover
bedeuten to mean
bedienen to serve; to operate

sich beeilen to hurry
beenden to finish
befehlen (+ *dat*) to order
sich befinden to be
begegnen (+ *dat*) to meet
beginnen to begin
begreifen to realize
behalten to keep, retain
behaupten to maintain
beherrschen to rule (over)
sich beklagen (über + *acc*) to
  complain (about)
bekommen to obtain
bemerken to notice
benachrichtigen to inform
benutzen to use
beobachten to watch
berichten to report
(sich) beruhigen to calm down
sich beschäftigen mit to attend to;
  to be concerned with
beschmutzen to dirty
beschreiben to describe
(be)schützen (vor + *dat*) to protect
  (from)
sich beschweren (über + *acc*)
  to complain (about)
besiegen to conquer
besitzen to own, possess
besprechen to discuss
bestehen (aus + *dat*) to consist (of),
  comprise
bestehen (auf + *dat*) to insist
  (upon)
bestellen to order
besuchen to attend, be present at,
  go to, visit
betreten to enter
beunruhigen to worry

(sich) bewegen to move
bewundern to admire
biegen to bend
bieten to offer
binden to tie
bitten to request
bitten um to ask for
bleiben to stay, remain
blicken (auf + *acc*) to glance (at),
  look (at)
borgen to borrow;
  jdm etw borgen to lend sb sth
brauchen to need
brechen to break
brennen to burn
bringen to bring, take
bummeln to wander; to skive
danken (+ *dat*) to thank
darstellen to represent
dauern to last
decken to cover
denken to think, believe
denken an (+ *acc*) to think of;
  to remember
denken über (+ *acc*) to think about;
  to reflect on
deuten (auf + *acc*) to point (to *or* at)
dienen to serve
diskutieren to discuss
drehen to turn; to shoot (*film*)
drucken to print
drücken to press, squeeze
durchführen to accomplish, carry
  out
durchqueren to cross, pass
  through
durchsuchen to search
dürfen to be allowed to
eilen to rush, dash

einfallen (+ dat) to occur
  (to someone)
einladen to invite
einrichten to establish, set up
einschalten to switch on
einschlafen to fall asleep
eintreten to come in
einwickeln to wrap (up)
empfangen to receive (person)
empfehlen to recommend
entdecken to discover
entführen to take away
enthalten to contain
(sich) entscheiden to decide
sich entschließen to make up one's
  mind
entschuldigen to excuse
sich entschuldigen (für) to
  apologize (for)
enttäuschen to disappoint
(sich) entwickeln to develop
sich ereignen to happen
erfahren to learn; to experience;
  erfahren von to hear about
erfolgreich successful
ergreifen to seize
erhalten to receive, get
sich erheben to rise
erinnern (an + acc) to remind (of)
sich erinnern (an + acc) to
  remember
erkennen to recognize
erklären to state; to explain
sich erkundigen (nach or über +
  acc) to inquire about
erlauben to allow, permit, let
erleben to experience
ermutigen to encourage
erobern to capture

erregen to disturb, excite
erreichen to reach; to catch
  (train etc)
errichten to erect
erschaffen to create
erscheinen to appear
erschrecken to frighten
erschüttern to shake, rock, stagger
erstaunen to astonish
erwachen to wake up (intransitive)
erwähnen to mention
erwarten to expect, await, wait for
erwidern to retort
erzählen to tell, explain
erziehen to bring up, educate
fallen to fall
fallen lassen to drop
falten to fold
fangen to catch
fassen to grasp; to comprehend
fehlen to be missing;
er fehlt mir I miss him
etw fertigmachen to bring sth
  about; to get sth ready
festbinden to tie, fasten
finden to find
fliehen (vor + dat, aus) to flee
  (from)
fließen (in + acc) to flow (into)
flüstern to whisper
folgen (+ dat) to follow
fordern to demand
fortgehen to go away
fortfahren to depart; to continue
fortsetzen to continue (transitive)
fragen to ask
sich fragen to wonder
sich freuen to be glad
führen to lead

füllen to fill
funkeln to sparkle
funktionieren to work (*of machine*)
sich fürchten (vor + *dat*) to
  be afraid *or* frightened (of)
geben to give
gebrauchen to use
gefallen (+ *dat*) to please;
  das gefällt mir I like that
gehen to go
gehorchen (+ *dat*) to obey
gehören (+ *dat*) to belong (to)
gelingen (+ *dat*) to succeed
gelten to be worth
genießen to enjoy
genügen to be sufficient
gern haben to like
geschehen to happen
gestatten to permit, allow
glauben (+ *dat*) to believe
glauben an (+ *acc*) to believe in
glühen to glow
gründen to establish
gucken to look
haben to have
halten to keep; to stop; to hold
  sich irren to be mistaken
halten für to consider (as)
handeln: es handelt sich um it is
  a question of
hängen to hang (up)
hassen to hate, loathe
hauen to cut, hew
heben to lift, raise
heimbringen to take home
helfen (+ *dat*) to help
herantreten an (+ *acc*) to approach
herausziehen to pull out
hereinkommen to enter, come in

hereinlassen to admit
herstellen to produce,
  manufacture
herunterlassen to lower
hineingehen (in + *acc*) to enter,
  go in (to)
hinlegen to put down
sich hinsetzen to sit down
hinstellen to put down
hinübergehen to go through;
  to go over
hinweisen to point out
hinweisen auf (+ *acc*) to refer to
hinzufügen to add
hoffen (auf + *acc*) to hope (for)
holen to fetch
horchen to listen
hören to hear
hüten to guard, watch over
interessieren to interest
sich für etw interessieren to be
  interested in sth
kämpfen to fight
kennen to know (*person, place*)
kennen lernen to meet, get to
  know
klagen to complain
klatschen to gossip
klettern to climb
klingeln to ring
klingen to sound
kochen to cook
kommen to come
können to be able (to)
kriegen to get, obtain
sich kümmern (um) to worry
  (about)
küssen to kiss
lassen to allow, let; to leave

laufen to run
leben to live
legen to lay
sich legen to lie down
Leid tun (+ dat) to feel sorry for
du tust mir Leid I feel sorry for you
es tut mir Leid I'm sorry
leiden to suffer; ich kann ihn nicht leiden I can't stand him
leihen to lend; sich (dat) etw leihen to borrow sth
leiten to guide, lead
lesen to read
lieben to love
liefern to deliver; to supply
liegen to be (situated)
loben to praise
löschen to put out
lösen to buy (ticket)
losmachen to unfasten undo, untie
loswerden to get rid of
lügen to lie, tell a lie
machen to do; to make
malen to paint
meinen to think, believe
mieten to hire, rent
mitbringen to bring
mitnehmen to take
mitteilen: jdm etw mitteilen to inform sb of sth
mögen to like
murmeln to murmur
müssen to have to (must), be obliged to
nachdenken (über + acc) to think (about)
nachsehen to check
nähen to sew

sich nähern (+ dat) to approach
nehmen to take
nennen to call, name
sich niederlegen to go to bed, lie down
notieren to note
öffnen to open
organisieren to organize
passen (+ dat) to suit, be suitable
passieren to happen
pflegen to take care of
plaudern to chat
pressen to press, squeeze
produzieren to produce
programmieren to program
protestieren to protest
prüfen to examine, check
rasieren to shave
raten (+ dat) to advise
räumen to clear away
reden to talk, speak
reinigen to clean, tidy up
reisen to go, travel
retten to save, rescue
riechen (nach) to smell (of)
rufen to call
sich rühren to stir
sagen (+ dat) to say (to), tell
säubern to clean
saugen to suck
schaden (+ dat) to harm
schallen to sound
schauen (auf + acc) to look (at)
scheinen to seem; to shine
schieben to push, shove
schießen to shoot
schlafen to sleep
schlafen gehen to go to bed
schlagen to hit, strike, knock, beat

sich schlagen to fight
(sich) schließen to close, shut
schneiden to cut
schnüren to tie
schreiben to write
schreien to shout, cry
schütteln to shake
schützen (vor + *dat*) to protect
(from)
schweigen to be silent
schwören to swear
sehen to see
sein to be
senken to lower
setzen to put (down), place, set
sich setzen to settle, sit (down)
seufzen to sigh
singen to sing
sitzen to sit, be sitting
sollen ought (to)
sorgen für to take care of, look after
sich sorgen (um) to worry (about)
sparen to save
spaßen to joke
spazieren gehen to go for a walk
sprechen to speak
stattfinden to take place
stecken to put, stick
stehen to stand
stehen bleiben to stop (*still*)
steigen to come *or* go up, rise;
to climb
stellen to put, place; to ask
(*a question*)
sterben to die
stimmen to be right
stoppen to stop (*transitive*)
stören to disturb
stoßen to push, shove

strecken to stretch
streiten to argue, fight
sich streiten to quarrel
stürzen to fall, crash
sich stürzen (in *or* auf + *acc*) to rush
or dash (into)
suchen to look for, search for
tanzen to dance
teilen to share, divide
teilnehmen (an + *dat*) to attend,
be present at, go to, take part (in)
töten to kill
tragen to carry; to wear
träumen to dream
treffen to meet; to strike (*transitive*)
trennen to separate; to divide
treiben to drive; to go in for
trocknen to dry
tun to do
so tun, als ob to pretend (that)
überlegen to consider, reflect
überraschen to surprise
überreden to persuade
übersetzen to translate
(sich) umdrehen to turn round
umgeben sein von to be
surrounded with *or* by
umgehen to avoid, bypass
umkehren to turn
umleiten to divert
umwerfen to overturn, knock over
unterbrechen to interrupt
unterhalten to support
(sich) unterhalten (über + *acc*)
to converse *or* talk (about);
to entertain
sich unterscheiden to differ,
be different
unterschreiben to sign

untersuchen to examine

sich verabreden to make an appointment

verbessern to improve

verbieten to forbid, prohibit

verbinden to connect; to bandage

verbringen to pass or spend (time)

verdecken to hide, cover up

verderben to spoil, ruin

verdienen to deserve

vereinigen to unite

vergessen to forget

sich verhalten to act, behave

verhindern to prevent

verlangen to demand, order

verlassen to leave

verleihen (an + acc) to lend (to)

verletzen to harm

verlieren to lose

es vermeiden, etw zu tun to avoid doing sth

vermieten to let, rent

versäumen to miss

(ver)schließen to lock

verschwinden to disappear, vanish

versehen (mit) to provide

versichern (+ dat) to convince, assure

versprechen to promise

(sich) verstecken (vor + dat) to hide (from)

verstehen to understand; was verstehen Sie darunter? what do you understand by that?

versuchen to try, taste, sample; to attempt to

verteidigen to defend

verteilen to distribute

verzeihen to pardon, forgive

vollenden to finish

vorbereiten to prepare

vorgeben to pretend

vorschlagen to suggest

(sich) vorstellen to introduce (oneself)

sich (dat) etw vorstellen to imagine sth

wachen to be awake

wachsen to grow

wagen to dare

wählen to elect; to choose

warten (auf + acc) to wait (for)

(sich) waschen to wash

wechseln to exchange; to change (money)

wecken to awaken, wake up (transitive)

wegnehmen to take off or away

sich weigern to refuse

weinen to cry

sich wenden an (+ acc) to apply to; to turn (to)

werden to become, grow, turn (out)

werfen to throw

wetten (auf + acc) to bet (on)

wiederholen to repeat

wiedersehen to see again

wischen to wipe

wissen to know

wohnen (in + dat) to live (in)

wohnen (bei + dat) to lodge (with), live (with)

wollen to want (to), wish (to)

sich wundern (über + acc) to wonder (at), be astonished (at or by)

es wundert mich I am surprised (at it)

das würde mich wundern!
  that would surprise me!
wünschen to wish
zählen to count
zeichnen to draw
zeigen to show, point
zelten to go camping
zerbrechen to break
zerreißen to tear up
zerstören to demolish, destroy
zerstreuen to scatter
ziehen to draw; to pull; to tug

zittern (vor + *dat*) to tremble (with)
zögern to hesitate
zugeben to confess, admit
zuhören (+ *dat*) to listen (to)
zumachen to close, shut (*transitive*)
zunehmen to put on weight
zurückkehren to come back, return
zurückkommen to go *or* come back
zurücksetzen, zurückstellen to
  replace
zweifeln to doubt
zwingen to force, oblige

ENGLISH
INDEX

The words on the following pages cover all of the
ESSENTIAL and IMPORTANT NOUNS in the book.